D0019052

LEFT OUT!

How Liberals Helped
Reelect George W. Bush

Joshua Frank
Foreword by Jeffrey St. Clair

Common Courage Press   Monroe, Maine

Library of Congress Cataloging-in-Publication Data is
available from publisher on request.
ISBN 1-56751-310-7 paper
ISBN 1-56751-311-5 hardcover

Common Courage Press
121 Red Barn Road
Monroe, ME 04951

207-525-0900
fax: 207-525-3068

www.commoncouragepress.com
info@commoncouragepress.com

First printing
Printed in Canada

CONTENTS

Part I

The Limits of Political Expediency

"How Could He?"

Senator Max Baucus and the Brutal Education of a Neophyte

At the naïve age of 18, while still in high school, I had the pleasure of flying across the country to Washington, DC, for a weeklong youth workshop on leadership and democracy. I remember the teary excitement I had, knowing I was about to meet both of my Montana senators. Back then I was a proud registered Democrat. Having joined the party only two months earlier, the prospect of rubbing shoulders with a veteran of my party, I thought, was sure to be the highlight of the visit.

I've been on a bad trip ever since, culminating in the realization that the Democrats, like the Republicans, are on the wrong side of justice. I had hoped this episode was an anomaly. But unfortunately the anomalies began to stack up, one after another, and a new reality soon set in. What I've learned since is maddening: integrity and the Democrats don't mix. What the Democratic Party represents today is a train wreck of ideals that has been derailed deliberately. Too bad I had to learn the hard way.

The swank décor of the hallways on the Hill in DC mesmerized me as I winded through the legislative chambers. The bright carpet and attractive young interns meandering around the foyers made me think that perhaps politics had its subtle rewards. My intrepid journey from wing to wing led me to the bustling office of the Montana Senator who would change my life, Mr. Max Baucus.

Max wasn't in, however, so a cheery office assistant led me

to a committee meeting that the Senator was attending. "It will be just a few minutes," she said, continuing to chat with me about the beauty and serenity of Montana. She had grown up in Great Falls or somewhere nearby, and missed the quiet open range and starry nights. I must have reminded her of what she was like before deciding to test the murky waters of Washington politics.

A few minutes later, Max scurried out and shook my hand as if I were the elected official he had traveled a thousand miles to meet. "So glad to finally meet you," he said. "How in the hell does he know who I am?" I thought. He didn't, of course. He was just politicking.

Max wasn't a good ol' boy like Senator Conrad Burns, his Republican rival from Montana, who said during his first campaign in 1988 that he would help single mothers by "[telling] them to find a husband." But Max was sleazy in his own right. His gaudy single-knot tie and wing-tip shoes caught my eye immediately. I remember wondering how long Mr. Baucus had been away from Big Sky Country. I didn't really care, though. He was the Democrat I had come to see.

I asked Max about Washington life, and we poked fun at Conrad Burns, whom I had met earlier in the day. Whereas Baucus' busy, over-packed office was full of citizens who seemed to care, Burns' quarters were filled with wide leather couches, southern blonde assistants, and trophy animals that hung on his plush papered walls. We joked about Burns' assistants who were advising him on how he should vote on specific legislation even though they had never even traveled to Montana. I thought to myself, "Man, Democrats really are a lot cooler than Republicans."

It didn't hurt that Max knew my uncle, who ran a little grocery store in Lockwood, a small town outside of the city where I grew up. It made me think Max was one of us, a regular guy who represented regular folks. I let the used car salesman attire slide; the guy was alright.

My trip ended soon thereafter. I had met some interesting people, seen a lot of monuments and museums, and was enthralled with how the system actually worked. At least I thought I understood how it worked. The runners, the lobbyists, the rookies, the senior congressional leaders, the reporters, and oh, those interns. I thought I had it down. I couldn't wait to get home to tell my family what I'd learned, whom I'd met, and how Senator Baucus knew my dad's brother. I was even contemplating the best way for me to help in his upcoming election campaign. As a Democrat enthusiast, I was much like Howard's Deaniacs, who canvassed my neighborhood daily with their cheeky grins and bouncy gaits.

It wasn't more than six months later that I was knocked to my senses. The fairytale had ended. I read in the newspaper that my buddy Max had supported the North America Free Trade Agreement (NAFTA) a few years prior. By then, I was interested in environmental issues and came across the effects of NAFTA and the senators who supported it. Baucus was at the top of the hit list. I couldn't believe it. I felt as if I had been two-timed by a corporate fraud who used phony idealism to woo me. I had been the victim of political date rape.

Upon further exploration, I learned that Baucus sat on influential congressional committees, including the Agriculture, Nutrition and Forestry, Environment and Public Works, and Finance and Joint Taxation committees. I learned how this man whom I had come to admire—for no real reason other than his bashing of a Republican—had succumbed to the interests of campaign contributors time and again. I found out how his seat on the Senate Finance Committee scored him bundles of cash from corporations I had never even heard of, including JP Morgan, Brown & Foreman, and Citigroup. I knew these guys weren't from Montana.

I also learned how my hero supported welfare reform, Fast

Track, and President Clinton's Salvage Rider Act, which raped the Montana forests I loved so dearly. And a year later in college I read an old article by Alexander Cockburn and Jeffrey St. Clair in *The Washington Post*, which disclosed how actor Robert Redford had campaigned for Baucus by dropping letters into the mailboxes of elite Hollywood liberals, hoping to entice them to donate money to the Montanan for his astute convictions for environmental justice.

But as St. Clair and Cockburn put it so poignantly, "Across the length and breadth of Congress, it is impossible to uncover a more tenacious front-man for the mining, timber, and grazing industries…it was Baucus who crushed the Clinton administration's timid effort to reform federal mining and grazing policies and terminate below-cost timber sales to big timber companies subsidized by the taxpayers."

I was outraged. "How could he…?!" I pondered. "If the Democrats aren't saving our natural resources, who the hell is…?!?"

That anger has festered in me to this day. Max Baucus may still be the most corporate-entrenched, conniving Democrat in Washington, and Montana has suffered tremendously as a result. High unemployment. A broken public school system. A degraded natural environmental. The exponential evaporation of the once hallowed family farm. Montana's hurting, and the Democrats—most certainly Baucus—don't seem to give a damn.

The dangling tassels on Max's fancy wing-tip shoes will forever irk me. Those tassels and his decorative silk tie should have been the first sign that this politician didn't represent Montana. He was, after all, literally clad in the interests of the out-of-state corporations that lined his thick campaign coffers. I have hated the pretentious Wall Street pin stripes ever since Baucus' sobering eye-opener.

I doubt that Max has ever hiked, let alone driven through

Montana's Yaak River basin, where a massive forest service sale has destroyed critical grizzly bear habitat. I'd bet he's never seen what the massive clear cuts have done to the region's ecosystem, as tributaries have turned a pale yellow from mud and debris. And I cannot imagine Baucus ever apologizing for the legislation he supported during the Clinton years that's to blame for it all. Many groups have challenged the illegalities of the outright pillage. But all of these suits have been defeated or dismissed because the salvage law gives the forest service "discretion to disregard entirely the effect on the grizzly bear." All this from the party to which I once belonged.

I can't fathom that Baucus has sat down and spoken with the hundreds of poor single mothers in rural Montana who can't afford to put their kids in daycare because they are forced to work at places like Wal-Mart where they earn little more than minimum wage. I am sure they'd love to tell him how grateful they are for their newfound careers and Clinton's welfare reform that put them to work. Unlike many progressives who are preoccupied with the war in Iraq and US foreign policy, these Montanans have more pressing concerns. They are turned off by politics because they have trouble keeping food in the fridge and buying holiday gifts for their kids. For most of us, it's a luxury to be politically active.

People continue to believe it's only the Republicans who have undermined everything progressives have fought for. I once believed this to be the case. I hated conservatives for their outright disregard for the little guy. But my short voyage out east as a teenager turned into a life lesson, teaching me that political affiliation means little when talking about real life consequences of compromising ideals.

Occasionally I wonder how my grandfather, who I am told was a staunch Democrat, would feel about all this mayhem. He wasn't a flashy man like the Democrats in Washington today, but a hardworking North Dakota farmer, who, as the story is told, even detested his neighbor for being what he called "one of those damned Republicans." Back then it was thought Democrats, although never progressive, stood for something genuine and were even elected into office because rural folk could discern the subtle difference between a donkey and an elephant.

Indeed there may still be minor variations, but when the donkey sprouts a trunk and grows big floppy ears, and the deep doo-doo we are all in smells like elephant shit, we've got problems no amount of political therapy will ever cure.

Whatever the Democrats call themselves, Mr. Baucus exposed the party's true face, and I now recognize a pachyderm when I see one.

***

The blatant narrowness of our mainstream political discourse and the continuing convergence of the two major parties in the US are such that the Democrats and other liberals actually helped reelect George W. Bush for a second term. I certainly don't buy that this election was stolen like so many liberals are convinced. But hypothetically, if election '04 was rigged, it should have never been close enough for Bush to steal. John Kerry should have won by a landslide. The Democrats simply failed to distinguish themselves on a host of critical issues.

To show just how narrow the Democratic debate is, I have dedicated Part I of *Left Out!* to the Howard Dean saga. You know him. For some time Dean, now the chair of the Democratic National Committee (DNC), appeared to be the candidate to take on Bush in the 2004 election. Many progressive voters believed that Dean was a true anti-war maverick. With his campaign bringing in unprecedented amounts of cash so early, he seemed unstoppable. A sort of semi truck through the snowdrifts, Dean had an active, if not overly eager, fan base.

But, whoa, hold on a minute there. How can it be that Democrats are a bunch of elephants when they have energetic insurgents like Howard Dean attempting to change the party from within? Dean *has* fostered change, as his success in winning a significant position in the DNC demonstrates. Sure, he didn't get the nomination for president, but he clearly represents a force within the establishment. Right?

Wrong.

Alas, by analyzing Howard Dean—who purportedly represents the liberal end of the respectable Democratic mainstream—we can clearly see just how much elephant blood races through the veins of the frail Democratic Party.

So why was Dean stopped during the presidential race if he wasn't even progressive to begin with? As I detail in Chapter Eight, the answer reveals a great deal about money and corporate power within the Democratic Party.

Nevertheless, following Kerry's embarrassing loss to Bush, Dean raced straight through the establishment gates screaming the mantra, "Change is on the way."

Many centrist Democrats feared Dean's positions were far too liberal and consequently opposed Dean's bid for the highly symbolic DNC chair. However, it wasn't Dean they were really afraid of, but rather his grassroots following. After all, the Democratic enterprise doesn't appreciate the competition from within its own ranks.

Later, however, the Washington Democrats and those DNC loyalists that voted for Dean realized the chair post would be the best place to shove the mangy pest. Slap ol' Dean in a position that has little to do with policy and much to do with corporate fundraising, they said. At least we'll get his grassroots cash along the way. And now the Democrats can declare, "Look, we have a progressive DNC chair! So it's okay now if we run someone like Joe Lieberman."

Roaming the blogs of Howard Dean's ardent supporters revealed mixed emotions about his decision to run for the DNC chair. Many Dean groupies were glad their man was attempting to take on the stalwarts of special interests, but others were upset that Dean's bid could jeopardize another race for the presidency in 2008.

"The President is always the leader of, and direction setter of, his party" wrote Rick Kolker of Ashburn, Virginia on Dean's popular website. "The DNC is what it is today because Bill Clinton made it that way. If you [would] run and [win] in 2008, you'd have the opportunity to remake the party in your image. Now that opportunity is lost."

Surely this lost opportunity was just what many Beltway players and Democratic leaders who supported Dean's DNC run had in mind for the doc. With Dean safely situated in a symbolic administrative role within the establishment, he is unlikely to cause as much of a ruckus. And Dean is very unlikely to run for president again in 2008. Plus, they claim, it'll shut him up. No more tangents. No more unscripted interviews. Dean will have to tout the party line at every turn. Which is all any of the Democratic elite ever wanted anyway.

Still it is important to analyze what Howard Dean represents within the broader context of the Democratic Party given the significant attention and support he garnered early on during the 2004 presidential race. We must recognize that genuine change is unlikely to come about even if waged by people like Dean and his enthusiasts.

While progressive-minded candidates may be able to infiltrate the Democrats at the local level, or even in the House, the assumption that the party can be *taken over* from the ground-up is a wasted proposition. The Democratic leadership in DC is simply too entrenched and too powerful, and Dean's spot at the DNC will not alter this disappointing pattern.

Besides, the Democrats have turned their backs on their base for decades and shifted the party far, far away from its historic roots, which were never radical to begin with. Why change now? And as you will see, had Dean been elected president, little would have changed.

As Thomas Frank, author of *What's the Matter with Kansas?: How Conservatives Won the Heart of America*, explained in a *New York Times* editorial following Bush's reelection, "This year voters claimed to rank 'values' as a more important issue than the economy and even the war in Iraq.

"And yet, Democrats still have no coherent framework for confronting this chronic complaint, much less understanding it. Instead, they 'triangulate,' they accommodate, they declare themselves converts to the Republican religion of the market, they sign off on NAFTA and welfare reform, they try to be more hawkish than the Republican militarists. And they lose. And they lose again."

Although he is right, Frank fails to admit that the Democrats are not the remedy for what ails us. The truth is, no Democrat will ever spark a populist uprising. We are past the point of no return. Change will only come when genuine pressure is levied at the Democrats from outside the party.

So what shall we do? If not Dean, then who? If not the Democrats, then what? However hopeless you may feel, there are still many possibilities.

I offer *Left Out!* as a preliminary step: we must see the Democratic Party for what it is, not for what it claims to be. Sure, we need electoral reforms, and undoubtedly we need more voices and choices in our political arena; third parties are imperative to a successful democracy.

We must continue to build force against *both* political parties during George W. Bush's second term. We cannot wait until six months before the election to wage battle, cave to the Democrats, and still maintain our credibility and integrity as a movement. The war is already under way; our work against a corrupt political system begins now.

Over the course of the next four years we are sure to hear some tepid New Democrats tell us time and again that the only way to beat the Republicans is to outflank them to the right. Take on their moral values and surpass their fanaticism. In fact, following the defeat of former Senate Minority Leader Tom Daschle of South Dakota, the Democrats quickly moved to replace him with Harry Reid, a right-wing Democrat from Nevada. Unlike Dean's new position, Reid's is quite influential in steering the policy course of the Democratic Party.

Reid, an admitted friend of George W. Bush and Dick Cheney, was being tapped for the position well before Daschle's defeat and quickly gained enough support to assure his appointment and confirmation. A conservative Mormon born and raised in Nevada, Reid could have run just as easily as a Republican when he first ran for office in 1982.

Reid is a strong opponent of privatizing Social Security, a position that has earned him the admiration of Ralph Nader, among others. But let us not be fooled into believing that Reid will offer up opposition to the Republican onslaught. His positions on abortion, war, civil liberties, family values, and health care mirror those of the Republicans.

In fact, his adversaries adore him for his conservative propensities. Fellow Mormon and right-wing Senator Orrin Hatch, a high-ranking Republican from Utah, said, "We all respect Senator Reid. He is one of the moderate voices around here who tries to get things to work."

NARAL, a pro-choice advocacy group, has awarded Reid a score of 29 percent on his report card. In other words, Senator Reid has voted against a woman's right to choose 71 percent of the time he has been given the chance.

Reid also has few qualms with expanding and implementing the racist death penalty. He voted in favor of rejecting racial statistics in death penalty appeals and voted "yes" on limiting the number of appeals allowed for federal death row inmates. And the list goes on.

As Reid consolidates power and drives the Democrats further right, we will learn a harsh lesson—that the Democrats are doing the Republicans' work, and helping to elect them along the way. This should become all the more apparent with each passing election cycle.

To counter this shift we must adopt the positions we know to be just, not those that we think will win elections. We have learned the hard way that the latter strategy is a losing one. It is not our job to concede—the Democrats have already done more than their fair share of that, and look how far it has gotten them. Reid, not surprisingly, will prove to be the wrong choice as Democratic leader in the Senate.

Progressives, leftists, libertarians, populists, and others must speak to the needs of the disenfranchised, the silenced, the forgotten. A living wage would be a great start. Sure, loads of religious zealots flocked to the polls to cast their votes for Bush this year out of fear of the legalization of gay marriage and destruction of family values, but don't you think millions more— some of the ones who stayed home in 2004 (40-42%)—would come out to vote if they actually believed voting would make a bit of difference in their daily lives?

Wouldn't a living wage bring out this vote? How about *real* universal health care? This by no means implies that other social justice concerns should be swept under the rug. On the contrary, there is no reason true populism cannot encompass labor rights as well as gay rights, for example (remember Harvey Milk?). The voice of the minority could one day be the voice of the majority. The key is to find a way to bring all these voices under the same tent with the same megaphone. However, the Democrats are not the ones handing out tickets to this celebration. In fact, they are turning people away at the door.

***

On Election Day night I propped my butt on an uneven stool at my local bar here in Albany, New York, ordered a beer, and watched the tallies come in. The majority of my pals perched next to me that dark night, it is safe to say, had not cast a vote for a candidate of either party in many years. And 2004 was no different. My friends were more concerned with the lotto numbers rolling in, which may be worth more to them than the national elections. Sad, but true.

These are working class folks. Blue collar to the bone. They are not lazy or apathetic, but realistic and wiser beyond any degree some lofty Ivy League institution could award them. They knew it didn't matter who won the presidential election. Change wasn't on the way, even if John Kerry promised so.

They certainly don't care much for Bush either. But his dishonesty does not come as a surprise. They don't trust politicians in general—especially some elite New Englander like Kerry, whose toughest decision is which of his mansions to escape to for the weekend.

And why should my friends, and millions of others like them, care? They are not going to vote unless they are given a reason. It's time we gave them one. Or two.

Let's keep up our movements. For it is social movements that have historically been responsible for radical social change in this country, from the forty-hour workweek to the end of the Vietnam War. We are the force behind those principled tides. Not presidents. Not political parties. Perhaps we can use Bush to our advantage and continue our fight against injustice at home and abroad for the next four years and beyond.

This book is written for those people out there who may agree with a guy like Ralph Nader but are deathly afraid of a man like George W. Bush, and consequently vote Democrat out of fear, rather than optimism. This is for Howard Dean's followers—people who want change and think the Democrats are capable of bringing it. This rationale in fact helped reelect the very man they so adamantly opposed.

So it is time for a wake-up call. I had mine some years back, thanks to Senator Baucus of Montana. Despite his pitfalls, Baucus deserves some credit for teaching me that Democrats aren't to be trusted any more than Republicans. In fact, as a thank you, I considered dedicating this little book to Max. He deserves it. Baucus surely influenced its political bent and my passion to expose the Democrats' fraud. Later, though, I realized what a huge waste this would be. Baucus, like so many of our other public servants, is not worth the recycled paper these words are printed on.

Senator Baucus will be in office until 2008, and he's not the only liberal imposter who will be. We are up against many. But if 2004 was our wake-up call, then the imposters themselves are also up against many—we, the people.

ACKNOWLEDGMENTS

There are many people I would like to thank for aiding in the completion of *Left Out!* First, some of the music that got me through: Tea for Julie, Yeah Yeah Yeahs, The Shins, Split Enz, Mike Watt, PJ, Bowie, Rilo Kiley, Dillard and Clark, Sleater-Kinney, KRS, Clampitt Gaddis & Buck, Radiohead, Robert Johnson, The Decembrists, just to name a few—thanks for the tunes, y'all.

My friend Jeffrey St. Clair, a fellow nature lover and the I.F. Stone of our fragile times, who believed in this project from the get-go. He first ran my Howard Dean columns at *CounterPunch* during the height of Dean's hysteric craze. Jeff believed the true story of Dean must be told, and I thank him for supporting my efforts, as well as his generous foreword herein. Greg Bates, my publisher at Common Courage Press, and all the other folks at CCP that helped out with this book, thank you much.

Like Jeff, Greg was there from the start, believing—even in the polluted "Anybody But Bush" environment—that these stories must persevere. He is a tireless editor as well, and I thank him for taking a youngster like me under his wing.

I also must thank my good friend Sunil Sharma, editor of DissidentVoice.org, for his unwavering encouragement and critiques throughout the process of putting together this manuscript. Merlin Chowkwanyun, whose wit is contagious and energy unmatched, for his additions and ideas. My radical comrades at LeftHook.org and PressAction.com, thank you, too. Mickey Z, your support mattered so much, thanks.

Marley Gaddis, thank you for your editing.

Laura Nathan perhaps worked closer with me than any other person during the writing process. Her editing skills are unparalleled, and I thank her immensely. Of course, any errors, factual or grammatical, fall at my feet alone.

I have to thank all the researchers and activists in Vermont and elsewhere that sifted though piles of articles and news clippings uncovering the authentic Howard Dean. You know who you are—thanks for your diligence.

To my wild beer-swilling friends out in Oregon, Montana, and Colorado, as well as my family scattered throughout the Midwest, thanks for putting up with my radical worldview, and cheers!

To my partner Jessica, who has stuck by me through the ups and downs and the twists and turns the world has tossed our way. She is intelligent, gorgeous, radiant, and has managed to put up with me despite the extensive hours I was glued to my iMac. I love her dearly.

Last, and most of all, my parents Dean and Laverne. They have supported me in every crazy scheme I have conjured up, every venture I undertook, and believed in me despite the odds (and my depleted bank account). They are by far the most inspirational people in my life. They are eternal optimists, and with love, I dedicate this book to them.

For my parents.

Foreword

Howard's End?

The Demise of the Democrats

By Jeffrey St. Clair

We find ourselves on the eroding down slope of empire. The titans have fallen. We are now ruled by minor princelings: Al Gore, George W. Bush, John Forbes Kerry, Howard Dean. These are the days of the dauphins.

A republic in name, we now rigidly follow the laws of political primogeniture. The slushy predictability of our current politics may well be our unraveling. The world awaits a change in fortune, betting on the collapse of the behemoth.

If this arthritic republic falls, it will crumble from within, like so many other overextended empires of old. The cracks are already showing up, unmaskable fissures in the foundations. The signs are abundant everywhere for those who still know how to read: in our phony politics, in our outsourced economy, in our looted and poisoned environment, in our corporatized culture that offers us bikini-clad women eating worms for entertainment, in our rotting schools, our burgeoning prison industry, our turnstile hospitals, our irredeemable racism, our executioners' gibbets where the most gruesome of political rituals are still played out in hiding. We are anxious to shed blood, but we can't stand to see it flow. Yet another birthmark of our perverted Puritanism.

F. Scott Fitzgerald, our most prescient writer, foretold it all in the novel he wanted to title *Under the Red, White, and Blue*. The great wheel of fortune has come full swing. The promise of the republic, the green light that lured so many to these forested shores, has been squandered. Worse: pilfered. The financial aristocrats that Thomas Jefferson and Benjamin Franklin warned us against at the very birth of this nation are more powerful than they have ever been. Jay Gould is a petty crook compared to the likes of Ken Lay and Dick Cheney. The rich are different. They crack things up and not only get away with it, but are glamorized and idolized for the damage they've done and the billions they've looted. We worship the beasts that devour us. The rest of us are left to scavenge the rubble, and our politics offer us false choices and few true champions.

Where is the resistance to this ruination?

Don't look to the powerbrokers of the Democratic Party. These days the creaky curators of the American left paint their opponents as maniacal demons. Hitler is the reflexive metaphor for any Republican. All the corroded left seems to know is the politics of hysteria. The purpose of this ritualized threat inflation is to make the pallid offerings of the Democratic Party seem credible. But Bush is not a fanged creature out of Bosch. He is stupid and dull, a banal frat boy, more Eichmann than Hitler. In his former Treasury Secretary Paul O'Neill's frank assessment, this President is blind, apathetic, and mute. Just a hearing aid shy of being our political version of The Who's "Tommy," minus the power chords. He doesn't, or can't, read the morning papers or briefing books. Condi Rice, the gorgon of the National Security Council, spoon-fed him what she felt he needed to know in small portions that could be easily regurgitated during his first four years. The real work is done by the coterie of neo-cons that swirl 'round him: Cheney, Rummy, Rove, Wolfowitz, and Card. In medieval times the cretinous sons of the elites were sent packing to the priesthood. These days they run for president, and everyone prays for the best.

So in the 2004 election cycle we were presented with Howard Dean, the latest incarnation of a maverick progressive. He is, of course, neither. But you can't mention that in mixed company. The image of Dean the pugilistic populist has already been manufactured and implanted into the popular consciousness. And everyone plays along, from the press to Dean's fellow Democrats, who yelp that he is a dangerous outsider bent on smashing the delicate balance of the Clinton years. Even Karl Rove slithers across the screen hissing homilies about the authentic Dean.

We must be thankful that Joshua Frank is willing to risk ridicule by the left establishment. His work is the first unfiltered excavation of the ideology of the Vermonter. The evidence unearthed here will unnerve many progressives who nurse their news from the nipples of *The New York Times*. But it's not too late for progressives to wean themselves. Frank's sober assessment offers us a nourishing shot at redemption, a chance to escape the political quagmire that has deadened the voices of opposition in this nation at the most tremulous hour of the republic.

The portrait Frank draws of Howard Dean isn't a resume of unparalleled mendacity, although Dean is revealed to be a gifted liar and craven politician untroubled by matters of conscience even when it means betraying friends and allies. No. The fragrance here is something worse. The smell of rot. Dean is shown to be a run-of-the-mill and mundane governor out of the Democratic mainstream. Beneath the layers of greasepaint, the Dean Minstrelsy Show is a political rerun underwritten by the same old sponsors. Not of George McGovern, God forbid, but of the same neo-liberal troupe that has cloned Gore, Lieberman, Kerry & Kerrey, Edwards, Breaux, Dodd, and the Clintons. Of course, Bill Clinton was freighted with a tragic flaw, which at least made his tenure somewhat, if not redeemable, at least diverting, though the play was much too long. Clinton could be hated. Dean, even in angry man mode, evokes only a dull throbbing of the cortex. This is what entropy feels like.

He is sour and surly, grouchy and privileged. Dean is the

Democrats' Bob Dole, sans the flinty Kansan's sense of humor, war record, and Viagra-fortified erections. Howard Dean seems about as erotically charged as Nixon.

He is a Yanqui, in the oldest and most disreputable sense of the term—a true scion of Wall Street and old money. It's one reason he was able to raise so much cash so quickly on the Internet. He's the Amazon.com of presidential candidates: a lot of money poured in early for insubstantial returns.

Dean ascended to power in the most self-consciously progressive state in the republic. A word or two about Vermont: I live in Oregon. Vermont could be our little sister state—only more homogenous and more uptight. It is blindingly white, wealthy, and snugly cocooned from fractious rhythms of the republic. Ralph Nader could be elected governor in the Green Mountain state. But Howard Dean is no Ralph Nader. Therein lies part of the truth about Dr. Dean.

* * *

Howard Dean was raised on Park Avenue, as the son of a Wall Street broker who held a lofty post at the Dean/Witter securities firm. As a youth, Dean spent his summers in East Hampton and went to elite private academies, including a stint at a boarding school in England. In 1967, Dean entered Yale. By all accounts, his tenure there was as unremarkable as that of George W. Bush. Unlike, say, Al Gore, then plotting the trajectory of his political career with Martin Peretz at Harvard, neither Dean nor Bush seem to have been particularly ambitious collegians.

Even at Yale in the late '60s, Dean was cautious, vaguely anti-war and pro-civil rights. But he refused to align himself with any particular movement on campus, saying that he "instinctively distrusted ideologues." But it's more likely he knew that any kind of radical association might impede the business career he was planning to pursue.

After Yale, Dean joined his father on Wall Street. He tried his hand at stock trading for a couple of years, made a bundle, got bored, and then went to medical school. Dean graduated from Albert Einstein Medical School in 1978, and fled to Vermont to undertake his residency. There he met his future wife, Judith Steinberg. They soon married and opened a medical practice together in Shelburne, Vermont.

Soon Dean grew bored with medicine and began to dabble in politics. In 1982, he was elected to the Vermont House of Representatives. By all accounts, it was a tenure undistinguished by any major accomplishment. Yet, four years later he ran for the position of lieutenant governor and won. He was elected to three consecutive terms of this largely ceremonial position. Then fate intervened. On August 14, 1991, Vermont's governor, Richard Snelling, was felled by a fatal heart attack. Dean sped to Montpelier upon hearing the news, and later that day he was sworn in as the new governor.

Dean's first major initiative as governor set the tone. The Vermont economy had been hobbled by recession, and Democrats in the state legislature were pushing a modest tax increase for social programs. The tax increase seemed ready to pass, then Dean intervened, siding with Republicans. Instead of raising taxes, Dean lowered them. It was a sign of things to come.

Dean governed Vermont from the middle-right. He fetishized balanced budgets, achieving the holy balance on the backs of the needy and the powerless. He pandered to the police, backing draconian drug laws and even lending support to the death penalty. He sided with Monsanto against environmentalists, organic farmers, and consumers. He trumpeted his own welfare reform plan that was as miserly as anything put forward by Tommy Thompson. A friend of nuclear power, Dean conspired with New England's other nuclear governors to unload the region's radioactive waste on a small and impoverished Hispanic town in west Texas called Sierra Blanca. And on and on.

Early in his campaign, his own mother ridiculed his presidential aspirations as "preposterous." Like George W., Dean was never his mother's favorite child, which may explain his tendency to throw political tantrums. These are the guys you really have to watch like a hawk.

After Dean vaulted to the front of a lethargic and uninspiring pack of competitors, he began making mistakes. It's so much easier to lope along as the underdog. Dean deadened much of his rustic appeal when he began to court the endorsements of party insiders—and losers at that: Al Gore, Jimmy Carter, Bill Bradley, Tom Harkin.

Then he famously solicited the votes of working-class southern rednecks, but he offered them nothing except a kind of thinly coded race-baiting. Dean lacks even the most basic rhetorical lingo to address the traumatic economic dislocations of the Bush/Clinton/Bush era. His economic agenda is scavenged from the wreckage of Tsongas and Bradley, offering only a kind of stern Yankee paternalism.

Aside from the Iraq war, the Dean schema is fetchingly elitist, gliding silently over the battered preterit of American society. Instead, Dean pushes policies sharply attuned to the appeasement of middle class anxieties, the nervy triangulated center. Hence the familiar concern about crime, drugs, health care costs (as opposed to universal care), education, and budget deficits. But with Dean the articulation of these centrist obsessions comes out sounding brittle and vaguely threatening. Clintonism shorn of empathy.

It's doubtful that many of Dean's former patients lament the fact that he abandoned his medical practice for politics. He has a stern bedside manner. This is a man, unlike Clinton, who displays little compassion for those in pain. Take medical pot. Despite Dean's confession of youthful encounters with the divine weed, the doctor opposes giving cancer and AIDS patients the right to smoke marijuana to ease their suffering. His health care plan was almost as stingy, a brand of Hillary-lite.

* * *

Then came Iowa. First, Dean lost the caucuses; then he lost his mind. I'm not talking about his Dexedrine-infused outburst following his defeat in this first primary, an election rigged by party bigwigs to tilt toward establishment favorites like Kerry and Edwards.

Of course, Dean made big mistakes. Fatal ones, as Frank exposes herein. For starters, he attacked Dick Gephardt in Iowa. Bad move. Dean didn't have to win Iowa outright. If he came in second to Gephardt, he would have still been perceived as the winner. After all, Iowa was Gephardt's backyard. But Dean got greedy. He wanted a sweep. He was baited into making a mortally false move. Dean dropped his mask, revealing an unappetizing visage. People didn't like it. In the meantime, affections of the voters drifted over to Kerry and Edwards.

After Iowa, the DNC powerbrokers snickered at the antics of Dizzy Dean. The Deaniac threat was never ideological. He is a pure neo-liberal. It came from the fact that he didn't owe the Clinton establishment anything. He raised his own money from the mysterious precincts of the virtual world. He was intemperate, perhaps ungovernable.

Soon the carrion birds were circling, stripping plank after plank of his campaign themes as if he were the corpse of Marsyas. The problem for Kerry and Clark and Edwards is that they were manufactured candidates, as processed as a GMO soybean. The vitality of Dean's campaign pulsed from its very unpredictability. He is an eccentric centrist, given to unscripted outbursts like a Prozac-taker gone off his meds.

The plantation masters of the party fear nothing more than unpredictability. That's one reason why they were so desperate to, as one senior Democratic congressman put it, "McGovern" him.

Yet, the election and its aftermath proved Dean to be a hollow man. Aside from Joe Trippi's innovative campaign strategy and Dean's hammering of Bush on the Iraq war, he did not have much to offer. Dean didn't know how to speak to working people, had little to say to greens, and insulted blacks. He wasn't all that angry, and he didn't know how to fight. Finally, he even surrendered his own signature issue, admitting that the war wasn't really a paramount concern to Democratic voters. Horrible, but true.

Then there was the pitiful spectacle of Dean dragging his wife, Judith, across the snowy cornfields and into the television studios. You could see how uncomfortable she was at each venue. There was a look of disgust on her face as she was pigeonholed into the role of dutiful wife by her own desperate husband and hypocritical news celebrities like the ghastly Dianne Sawyer, who had a dalliance with Henry Kissinger when she was a debutante in the Nixon White House. Dean lost the election (and his credibility) right there.

Then it went straight downhill. Rarely has a front-running campaign, freighted with cash and an army of devoted volunteers, capsized so suddenly with so little provocation and not even the whiff of inner campaign scandal. The dull demise of Howard Dean makes one long for the salacious pleasures of Gary Hart, Donna Rice, and Monkey Business.

There were more problems. His TV ads were inept. Joe Trippi got too much credit for building the Dean phenomenon and not enough blame for orchestrating a terrible series of commercials, which turned off voters across the Hawkeye State. Trippi walked away from the wreckage with millions for his firm and acted as if his fingerprints weren't on the carnage.

Dean drove the final nail into his coffin by replacing Trippi with Roy Neel. Neel is a telecom lobbyist who exploited his cachet with the Clinton White House to maneuver the atrocious Telecommunications Act through Congress in 1996, one of the greatest corporate giveaways of the Clinton/Gore era. Neel is the same Beltway savant who advised Gore not to contest his own election. Neel's function wasn't to resuscitate Dean's campaign but to ease it into extinction, limiting the damage to the Democratic Party and, if he could, rehab Dean's reputation among party loyalists. Dean went along with it all like a beaten puppy. The man has no pride.

By February 18, it was all over. The plug was pulled on the Dean campaign. Having burned through money faster than Michael Jackson goes through lawyers, Dean found himself deep in debt. To bail his way out, Dean set up Democracy for America, a holding pen for Deaniacs to keep them from eloping to Naderland. It even won the endorsement of DNC kingpin Terry McAuliffe. The circle had been squared.

In mid-May 2004, Howard Dean joined John Kerry for a triumphant campaign swing through the Pacific Northwest. They held hands, played hearts on the campaign bus, gushered effusions of praise on each other. There was no unsettling talk of the war or the Patriot Act or the sadistic horrors of Abu Ghraib that had played out that very week. Instead, the candidate purred to the press about a "Kerry and Dean" administration. Dean smiled, halfway to paying off his staggering campaign debts. Since he had surrendered his run for the nomination, over 750 US troops and more than 5,000 Iraqis had perished. Kerry vowed to keep the troops in Iraq for another four years. And the putative anti-war candidate said nothing of it. Perhaps Dean is future establishment material after all.

Chapter One

Howard Helped Bush?

The Politics of Deceit

How could Howard Dean—the man trounced by establishment Democrats—be one of the liberals that actually helped reelect George W. Bush? If anything, Dean appears to be an insurgent who might have led his party in a better direction and actually won the presidency by offering an alternative to government as usual. Nonetheless, a closer examination of this "exception to the rule" sheds light on the limits of the Democratic Party and exposes their inability to offer genuine alternatives.

In his early campaign speeches, Dean exclaimed, "You don't know me, but you will." How right he was. Indeed, many, including elite circles of Washington Democrats who were already putting their resources behind the candidacy of John F. Kerry, had not heard much of the former Vermont governor. But Dean thought he was ready to take the insiders on, full-throttle. The feisty Vermonter entered the race for president on June 23, 2003, and immediately laid out his strategy for challenging George W. Bush and his band of neoconservative cronies. "You've got the power to take back Washington!" he yelled. And folks listened.

Even before Dean officially announced his intentions to run for president, he seemed to have his finger on the pulse of the Democratic underground. He knew that hostility among his party's grassroots had all but boiled over by March of 2003, when top "liberals" in DC caved in and endorsed the Bush administration's invasion of Iraq. As opponents of the US-led war on Iraq took their grievances to the streets across the country, hundreds of young Democratic enthusiasts handed out Dean campaign propaganda to their protesters-in-arms. For Dean's base, this was a golden opportunity to spread the word that Howard was not only going to run for president, but that he also opposed the invasion of Iraq.

Internet Might

These progressives latched onto Dean's insurgent candidacy quickly, and, luckily for him, they all had cash and Internet access. Joe Trippi, Dean's ingenious campaign manager, and the campaign's outreach webmasters, Matthew Gross and Zephyr Teachout, ran his web sensation. Trippi, an aeronautical engineering student in college with a former career in computer software and the experience of six presidential campaigns to his name, brought technological expertise to his managerial post. And like the Internet bubble of the 1990s, Dean's website literally took off in a matter of weeks. For the first time a presidential campaign was using the far-reaching capabilities of the Internet to spread the word about its candidate. With the help of online forums and Web logs (blogs), the campaign enabled like-minded people to convene and communicate with one another about the Dean campaign and vent frustration about the egregious policies of the first four years of the Bush junta.

In an interview with Lawrence Lessig, Trippi said of the Dean blog, "[I think] there's a sense of community that forms around the blog. That's really what the net is about. It's about building a community. There may be zillions of communities within the net, but you know, your own community builds around that blog." Dean, meanwhile, could not have been happier about his campaign's early success: "We fell into this by accident," admitted Dean. "I wish I could tell you we were smart enough to figure this out. But the community taught us. They built our organization for us before we had an organization."

On January 14, 2005, staff writers for the *Wall Street Journal* reported that the Dean campaign had in fact paid Internet "bloggers" as consultants so that they would support Dean for president. As the *Journal* contended, "Zephyr Teachout, the former head of Internet outreach for Mr. Dean's campaign, made the disclosure earlier this week in her own Web log, Zonkette. She said 'to be very clear, they never committed to supporting Dean for the payment—but it was very clearly, internally, our goal.' ... The partisan Democratic political bloggers who were hired by the Dean campaign were Jerome Armstrong, who publishes the blog MyDD, and Markos Zuniga, who publishes DailyKos. DailyKos is the ninth most linked blog on the Internet."

However, Dean's campaign wasn't propelled by blogs alone. Meetup.com, an Internet site that enables the organization of events for groups and other social networks, also played a pivotal role. With this organizing tool, the Dean for America campaign was able to bring together and organize supporters in cities throughout the US. In the spring of 2003, Dean attended his first Meetup event in New York City, where 300 loyal followers were in attendance. Amazed with the turnout, Dean knew that the vitality of his campaign involved bringing together like-minded people like the large NYC group.

By late March 2003, the Dean campaign was the most successful Meetup group ever, far outnumbering the forthcoming presidential aspirants with over 16,000 members. All this before Dean had even officially announced his own candidacy. By late 2003, that number soared; over 140,000 Dean supporters ("Deaniacs," as they called themselves) had joined Meetup and attended Dean campaign events, typically held on a weekly basis at a local café or pub, where supporters met to discuss how to spread the populist word on the Vermonter.

Trippi and his gang were running a successful one-of-a-kind campaign. In a Wired.com interview in early January 2004, Dean avowed, "A lot of the people on the net have given up on traditional politics precisely because it was about television and the ballot box, and they had no way to shout back," he said. "What we've given people is a way to shout back, and we listen—they don't even have to shout anymore."

Unlike his rivals in the campaign to unseat Bush, Dean claimed to actually be in tune with his community of faithful supporters, who by June of 2003 had raised over $10.5 million for his campaign. Bringing in over $15 million dollars in small online donations—which typically averaged a meager $25 a pop—Dean broke the record for money raised by a single Democrat in one period by the presidential race's third quarter. Dean's crusade was in full flight. "This is a campaign that no one has ever seen before!" Trippi exclaimed.

It was the making of a new wave of democratic participation—call it "credit card activism"—where tech-savvy liberals latched onto Howard Dean's unorthodox campaign while he challenged the Iraq war and took on the Democratic establishment (Democratic National Committee, DNC, and the Democratic Leadership Council, DLC) by raising bundles of cash outside the Democrats' normal corporate circles. When the online activist organization MoveOn.org held their mock primary in late June 2003, the Dean campaign received an added boost, receiving financing from their own broad membership base. Echoing the beliefs of these liberals, Dean felt that the DC insiders were taking their party "too far to the right." And they were none too happy.

"I have come to believe that a large part of why the DLC attacks Howard Dean so vehemently has a lot more to do with the power of what they're saying this campaign is about," said Trippi during Dean's summer peak. "They're not real thrilled with it."

To be sure, Dean was taking on the harlots of special interest—read: John Kerry and former DNC chair Terry McAuliffe—for their support of Bush's war while ignoring his fellow peace candidate Dennis Kucinich time and time again. Slyly borrowing a line from the late Senator Paul Wellstone, Dean proclaimed that, unlike the other candidates, he truly represented "the Democratic wing of the Democratic Party." Dean was certainly empowered by his massive cyber support, and despite the Beltway Democrats' response, the media had no choice but to cover his ardent campaign.

The story of how Howard Dean went from a supposed attacker, battering down the stodgy gates of the Democratic institution, to an insider hell-bent on weakening the party, further explicates that he and his party in fact helped reelect George W. Bush. What follows should serve as a dramatic warning of what the liberal end of the Democratic Party actually looks like, and why such a slight alternative to the Republican agenda will not win important elections.

Media Barrage

When the national media finally began to track the Dean spectacle, they were unsure of how to respond. Dean's style seemed fuming and visceral—he wasn't polished; he wore old suits, skinny ties, and penny loafers. He was not "presidential" by traditional TV standards. After a speech given by Dean, *The Washington Post* introduced the presidential hopeful with the following unbecoming portrait: "Howard Dean was angry. Ropy veins popped out of his neck, blood rushed to his cheeks, and his eyes, normally blue-gray, flashed black, all dilated ..."

Republican attack dogs quickly pounced on such caricatures. And Dean soon became the beloved soft target for right-wing pundits like the fat, racist, pill-popping Rush Limbaugh, who claimed that Dean was not only a fanatic but also a crazy Maoist, out of touch with the *real* America. In fact, Rush claimed Dean wasn't portrayed as liberal enough by the corporate media. "Have you noticed how some in the press are starting to say Howard Dean is not that liberal?" Limbaugh barked on his popular radio show. "Keep a sharp eye out for that because the left knows that being a far left, progressive liberal is a killer, so they're going to try to paint the picture of Dean as a moderate."

Of course, it was pure trash, as Howard Dean touted his centrist platform time and again while trouncing along the campaign trail. "I think it's pathetic I'm considered a left-wing liberal," Dean was quoted as saying in a 2003 *Washington Post* article. "It just shows how far to the right this country has lurched."

Not all coverage was negative, however. In the summer of 2003, Dean graced the covers of *Time*, *Newsweek*, and *Rolling Stone*. While the features run in these three magazines were by-and-large honest portrayals of the ex-governor, they failed to analyze his tenure in Vermont critically. Instead, most pieces in the corporate press were character assassinations, and not overly critical of his policy positions. Some pieces on the left, including several articles I wrote, were critical of Dean's politics, not personal attacks of the Fox News variety.

On the flip side, many in the liberal establishment praised the governor. Various columnists like *The Nation*'s prosier pundit Eric Alterman defended Dean in late 2003, writing, "Saddam Hussein may be out of his spider hole, but Washington's real enemy is still at-large. His name: 'Howard Dean'—and nobody in America poses a bigger threat to the city's sense of its own importance," Alterman snarled. *"New Republic* writer Michelle Cottle returned from maternity leave to find Washington fit for a 'Tarantino-style blood bath,' with the Democratic front-runner cast as a 'paleoliberal... a heartless conservative...too naïve to beat Bush...too politically cynical to trust...a Stalinist...[and] a neofascist [who] kills babies and drinks their blood ... Dean has some problems, no doubt, but the pundits hardly seem to notice that George W. ("You can't distinguish between Al Qaeda and Saddam when you talk about the war on terror") Bush cannot pretend to defend deceiving the nation into war anymore."

Other liberals, enticed by Dean's alleged tenacity, praised

him for offering an alternative—albeit, as you'll read later, an "alternative" based mostly on rhetoric and largely unsupported by substantive evidence. But respected author and syndicated columnist Molly Ivins, who recognized Dean was no liberal, wrote in support of his efforts nonetheless, "I went up to Vermont and talked to a bunch of liberals there. They all said Howard Dean is no liberal. Funny, that's what Howard Dean says, too. And indeed, he isn't, but in politics, everything's relative."

Veteran political author William Greider, who at one point played an advisory role in the Dean campaign, wrote of the governor's demeanor in an article entitled "Why I'm For Dean." "The press corps has not had much experience with Democrats of this type, so reporters read Dean's style as emotional, possibly a character flaw. He reminds me of olden days when Democrats were a more contentious bunch, always fighting noisily among themselves and often with creative results ... The guy is a better politician than the insiders imagined, indeed better attuned to this season than they are."

As these well-known commentators embraced the Dean saga, the corporate media continued to lambaste him for his personality quarks and on-stage slip-ups. Some conspiratorial Deaniacs contended that it was purely a reactionary fight because Dean was speaking out against media consolidation. Others claimed it was meant to paint Dean as unelectable. "The former Vermont governor remains the front-runner among Democratic voters," Eric Boehlert wrote for Salon.com in January of 2004. "[H]e's gotten increasingly caustic treatment from the media, which has dwelled on three big themes—that Dean's angry, gaffe-prone and probably not electable—while giving comparatively far less ink to the doctor's policy and political prescriptions that have catapulted him ahead of the Democratic field." All this unsavory media coverage months before the first caucus vote was cast in Iowa.

Endorsing a Loser

In early November 2003, the two largest labor unions in the country—the American Federation of State, County and Municipal Employees, and the Service Employees International Union—pledged to back Howard Dean, providing a striking blow to the labor famous Richard Gephardt's lackluster campaign. Made up of 3 million strong, the unions' bandwagon support seemed to solidify Dean as the man to beat.

Then, in a bold move in early December, former Vice President Al Gore endorsed Dean for America. Gore, invigorated by his 2000 loss—er, win—was chastised for turning his back on the DLC and his former running mate, Connecticut Senator Joseph Lieberman. And in January 2004, just before the first Iowa caucus, Tom Harkin, the veteran Democratic Senator from the Hawkeye state, rolled up his sleeves and gave Dean a spirited endorsement. "For me, the candidate that rose to the top as our best shot to beat George W. Bush and to give Americans the opportunity to take our country back," Harkin cheered, "That person is Governor Howard Dean!"

Things were rolling along well for Howard. Iowa's race was tightening, but he kept a healthy lead in the polls. Nobody could ignore his campaign now. He was the real deal. Even so, what was Howard Dean really about, other than his gang of young liberals and a phat $47 million bankroll? Aside from sound bites and his scorching campaign speeches across the country, what did Dean's record in Vermont actually reveal? More importantly, why did Howard Dean plummet so fast? What inner-workings were responsible for his demise?

The stories that follow unravel the authentic record of Howard Dean's reign in Vermont, as well as his positions on critical issues while campaigning for the presidency of the United States. In this sketch, you will not find a radical leftist, or even a liberal in most cases—which indeed makes Dean's story that much more interesting.

Why did Democratic insiders bury Dean, despite his DNC patronage and conservative philosophy? If anything, the accounts on the subsequent pages support Dean's own assessment of the political landscape in America and show just how far to the right the parade of donkeys in America has lurched. And unbeknownst to Dr. Dean, he may well be the whistleblower of the bona fide Democratic establishment that was unknowingly working in favor of Republican interests. Indeed, Dean's campaign exposed us all to the dirty tricks the Democrats will use in order to sabotage threats to party business.

Chapter Two

Nuanced War Positions

Dean was Never Anti-War

"Unilateral action is not appropriate unless there is an
imminent threat to the United States."

Howard Dean, The Nation, March 31, 2003

oward Dean was labeled by Republicans—and much
of the mainstream media—as the anti-war candidate,
representing the left wing of the Democratic Party. But while Dean
dodged the draft during the 1960s (he had a bum back) to avoid
serving in Vietnam, the conscientious objections of his youth were
not representative of his policy stance once he became involved
in national politics.

Looking back, Dean had a long pro-war history. He praised
the first Gulf War, NATO's intervention in Bosnia, Clinton's
bombings of the Sudan and Iraq. Dean even went so far as to write
President Clinton a letter praising his foreign policy in 1995, as
the US planned a brutal air attack on Serbia, bringing death and
destruction to civilians and the infrastructure that provided their
only life support.

Dean confessed to President Clinton: "I think your policy up
to this date has been absolutely correct ... Since it is clearly no
longer possible to take action in conjunction with NATO and the
United Nations, I have reluctantly concluded that we must take
unilateral action." According to most post-war accounts, US air
bombardment left the Serbian military relatively unscathed, while
ethnic cleansing and violence increased drastically.

Noam Chomsky in May of 1999 argued in *Z Magazine* that
the Clinton Administration began NATO's bombing precisely

because it would accelerate misery and curb democracy in that region:

> In the preceding year, according to Western sources, about 2,000 people had been killed in the Yugoslav province of Kosovo and there were several hundred thousand internal refugees. The humanitarian catastrophe was overwhelmingly attributable to Yugoslav military and police forces, the main victims being ethnic Albanian Kosovars, commonly said to constitute about 90 percent of the population. After three days of bombing, according to the UN High Commissioner for Refugees, several thousand refugees had been expelled to Albania and Macedonia, the two neighboring countries. Refugees reported that the terror had reached the capital city of Pristina, largely spared before, and provided credible accounts of large-scale destruction of villages, assassinations, and a radical increase in generation of refugees, perhaps an effort to expel a good part of the Albanian population. Within two weeks the flood of refugees had reached some 350,000, mostly from the southern sections of Kosovo adjoining Macedonia and Albania, while unknown numbers of Serbs fled north to Serbia to escape the increased violence from the air and on the ground.

Nonetheless, Governor Dean supported Clinton's deadly policy without a wince of shame.

Candidate Dean was no different. Despite voicing his opposition to Bush's war when he entered the race for the White House, Dean never wholeheartedly opposed overthrowing Iraqi president Saddam Hussein. In September 2002, Dean had announced that if Saddam failed to comply with the demands of the United Nations, the US reserved the right to "go into Iraq." Dean claimed he would gladly endorse a multilateral effort to destroy Saddam's regime. In fact, as we will discuss shortly, Dean wasn't even opposed to a unilateral effort lacking the support of the UN, NATO, or the European Union.

On CBS's *Meet the Press* in July 2003, Dean told Tim Russert that the United States must increase its pressure on Saudi Arabia and Iran. "We have to be very, very careful of Iran" because President Bush "is too beholden to the Saudis and the Iranians," he explained. But later in the broadcast, he conceded, "I support the President's War on Terrorism." Dean even went so far as to tell Russert: "I believe that we need a very substantial increase in troops. They don't all have to be American troops. My guess would be that we would need at least 30,000 and 40,000 additional troops." Sounds like John Kerry at the height of campaign 2004.

In a New York primary debate two months later, Dean elaborated: "We need more troops. They're going to be foreign troops [in Iraq], not more American troops, as they should have been in the first place. Ours need to come home." Dean, it seems, would have the disorder in Iraq go on at all costs, though he wasn't quite sure whose soldiers should do the occupying.

When Dennis Kucinich grilled Dean during that same debate about Bush's $87 billion Iraq package, Dean claimed that he would support it since "we have no choice ... we have to support our troops." So do we support our troops by bringing them home, or by financing the occupation? The self-proclaimed anti-war candidate never clarified.

Prior to the invasion of Iraq, Dean deemed the Afghanistan war vital to ending terrorism. Of course, this logic was ill-founded as the human toll was enormous, and bin Laden was never apprehended.

In an October 8, 2001 op-ed column in *The New York Times*, Middle Eastern scholar Fawaz A. Gerges, a professor at Sarah Lawrence College, pointed to the real aims that motivate the US war drive. Describing a conference of Arab and Muslim organizations held a week before in Beirut, Gerges wrote:

Most participants claimed that the United States aims at far more than destroying Osama bin Laden's Al Qaeda organization and toppling the Taliban regime. These representatives of the Muslim world were almost unanimously suspicious of America's intentions, believing that the United States has an overarching strategy which includes control of the oil and gas resources in Central Asia, encroachment on Chinese and Russian spheres of influence, destruction of the Iraqi regime, and consolidation of America's grip on the oil-producing Persian Gulf regimes.

Many Muslims suspected the Bush administration of hoping to exploit this tragedy to settle old scores and assert American hegemony in the world.

The governor also failed to critique the misguided foreign policy paradigms of the US leading up to and following the September 11 attacks. Dean believed that in order to fight terror, America must use an "iron fist" approach. Aggression, according to Dean, was the only way to challenge the cycle of terror plaguing our vulnerable world.

More fervent observers of Bush's foreign policy will notice that Dean's hollow position on the war on terrorism did not differ drastically from that of the Bush Administration's. In fact, with the exception of the rhetoric used by their proponents, the two strategies seem to be virtually identical.

Preemption and Meager Opposition

On April 9, 2003, Dean all but endorsed Bush's preemptive doctrine. Though Dean didn't join in the hawks' celebration of Bush's "liberation of Iraq" that day, he stressed the necessity of pressuring Iran and North Korea, saying he would not rule out the use of military force to do so. As Glen Johnson of the *Boston Globe* quoted Dean as saying on April 10, 2003, "Under no circumstances can we permit North Korea to have a nuclear program … nor, under any circumstances, can we allow Iran to have nuclear weapons."

By conceding that effective containment of such rogue states may necessitate the use of force, Dean endorsed a preemptive creed that has had the effect of isolating the United States from the international community. It goes without saying that by embracing the doctrine, Dean's foreign policy vision would not have reversed this trend.

Despite the similarities between Dean and Bush on pre-emption, many anti-war liberals eagerly embraced Dean's nuanced position against the Iraq war. As he told National Public Radio political correspondent Mara Liasson, "There are two groups of people who support me because of the war … One are the people who always oppose every war, and in the end, … I probably won't get all of those people." The other group, Dean said, were constituents who supported his Iraq position because he spoke out early and "represented the facts."

But this so-called "representation of the facts" demands closer examination, as it contradicts Dean's "anti-war" label.

According to Dean, had Bush produced accurate data proving that Saddam harbored weapons of mass destruction, Dean would have supported the unilateral invasion of Iraq. As Ron Brownstein reported in *The Los Angeles Times* on January 31, 2003, Dean said, "[I]f Bush presents what he considered to be persuasive evidence that Iraq still had weapons of mass destruction, he would support military action, even without UN authorization." However, Dean failed to note that the UN Charter forbids member countries from attacking another country except in self-defense.

Just one month later, Dean alienated his anti-war base, admitting in a February 20 Salon.com interview: "[I]f the UN in the end chooses not to enforce its own resolutions, then the US should give Saddam 30 to 60 days to disarm, and if he doesn't, unilateral action is a regrettable, but unavoidable, choice." Dean, had he taken a legitimate antiwar position, would have argued that when the US puts itself above international law, as it did by disregarding the UN Charter, it further encourages other nations to do the same.

As Dean initially articulated his muddled position on Iraq, Danny Sebright, one of the premier architects of Bush's Afghanistan conflict, played puppeteer behind the theatrical curtain. According to Sean Donahue, the Project Director of the Corporations and Militarism Project of the Massachusetts Anti-Corporate Clearinghouse, Sebright constructed and wrote Dean's early statements on war. At that time, Sebright worked under Donald Rumsfeld at the Pentagon as the Director of the Executive Secretariat for Enduring Freedom. As Donahue wrote in an October 30, 2003 article on *CounterPunch*:

> When Sebright left the Pentagon in February of 2002, he went to work for his old boss, former Secretary of Defense William Cohen, at the Cohen Group, a Washington-based consulting company. The firm uses its political connections to help companies obtain contracts with the Pentagon and with foreign governments. While it is discreet about its clientele, the Cohen Group does list some of its successes on its website—a list that includes helping to negotiate arms sales to Latin American and Eastern European countries, and advis[ing] and assist[ing] [a] US company in working with US Government officials and the Coalition Provisional Authority in securing major contracts related to Iraq reconstruction.

The fact that a close Dean advisor worked for a consulting firm involved in pitching contracts for reconstruction projects in Iraq raises questions about the true motives of Dean's support for the President's $87 billion Iraqi reconstruction program.

Dean's choice of Sebright as an advisor shows how little

difference there actually was between Dean and the Bush administration on the issue of the Iraq war.

Based on the statements made by Dean after announcing his campaign in the summer 2003, it appears that he only opposed the war in Iraq because he didn't believe the Bush administration had proven that Iraq posed an "imminent threat" toward the United States. For starters, Dean forgot that an attack by United States only inflames more anti-U.S. sentiment, feeding right into bin Laden's own rhetoric, which may stimulate future attacks by fundamentalist extremists against the US abroad and at home.

During this prelude to war, the Pentagon also estimated that an invasion of Iraq could lead to the deaths of 10,000 innocent civilians (most sources now say this has been exceeded substantially). The CIA during this period also reported that if Saddam did happen to possess biological weapons, he was more likely to use them in defense if attacked by the US, putting even more Iraqi civilians and US troops at grave risk.

Finally, Dean should have realized that there was no guarantee that a new regime in Iraq would make life any better for the Iraqi people, who already lived under a tyrannical dictator. Or that Iraq would be any friendlier to the US than Saddam was. Dean should have also noted that the Taliban were once our allies in Afghanistan, but now our enemy. Would Iraq's new regime prove to be the same?

So certainly there are many other reasons Dean should have raised opposition to the Iraq war. However, by failing to do so, it became strikingly clear that Dean was not an "antiwar" candidate. The fact is, Howard Dean proved he was just another candidate from the Democratic mainstream whose position on Iraq was not grounded on a philosophical aversion to war. On the contrary, Dean's opposition was political in nature.

Chapter Three

Defending Zionism and War Profiteering

The Same Old Bag

"At one time the Peace Now view was important, but now Israel is under enormous pressure. We must stop terrorism before peace negotiations."

Howard Dean, The Forward, November 22, 2002

Howard Dean's fickle stance on war does not end here. The October 2003 issue of *The Jewish Week* quoted Dean as saying that he had been very clear in his support for "targeted assassinations" of alleged Palestinian terror suspects. He believed these men were "enemy combatants in a war," adding, "Israel has every right to shoot them before they can shoot Israelis." This position bears a striking resemblance to that of both Presidents Bush and Clinton.

Why was Dean's position, like that of Bush and Clinton, wrong? From the 1948 war to the proposal to settle the whole of the Occupied Territories, Israel has always been associated with the policy of expelling Palestinians from the land—an act that is frighteningly similar to the Nazi objective during the Second World War to round up and clear all the Jews from Europe to provide "Lebensraum" for the citizens of Germany.

Dean's stance on the Israel/Palestine conflict may well be explained by the fact that his campaign fundraiser, Steven Grossman, was the former director of the American Israel Public Affairs Committee (AIPAC). The most influential pro-Israel lobby in the United States, AIPAC is committed to, amongst other things, defending Israeli Prime Minister Ariel Sharon and his Likud Party's every mishap.

"In the 1980s, AIPAC set up the Washington Institute for Near East Policy (WINEP) as a pro-Israeli alternative to the Brookings Institution, which it perceived to be insufficiently supportive of Israel. WINEP has largely followed AIPAC into pro-Likud positions, even though its director, Dennis Ross, is more moderate," writes Juan Cole, a distinguished history professor at the University of Michigan, in Antiwar.com on August 30, 2004.

"[Ross] is a figurehead, however, serving to disguise the far right character of most of the position papers produced by long-term WINEP staff and by extremist visitors and 'associates' (Daniel Pipes and Martin Kramer are among the latter).

"WINEP, being a wing of AIPAC, is enormously influential in Washington. State Department and military personnel are actually detailed there to 'learn' about 'the Middle East!' They would get a far more balanced 'education' about the region in any Israeli university, since most Israeli academics are professionals, whereas WINEP is a 'think tank' that hires by ideology."

What does that ideology entail? How about support for the current wall being erected by Israel to keep Palestinians at bay, as well as Israeli settlements in the West Bank, support for a nuclear program in the country, as well as billions in US aid? All this despite the numerous UN resolutions Israel has broken with their dealings of occupied territories of Palestine, including UN Resolution 1402, which demands that Israel withdraw its military from all Palestinian cities at once.

Nevertheless, Dean's defense of AIPAC and Ariel Sharon, whom Bush has called a "man of peace," mirrored the sentiments of many of Washington's most influential Zionist strategists.

For instance, Richard Perle, the ex-Chairman of the Defense Policy Board who was influential in advising the Bush administration on invading Iraq, certainly would have corroborated Dean's comments in the December 5, 2003 issue of *The Jerusalem Post*. An article in that issue quoted Dean as saying, "Israel is a democracy, [and] the only democracy aside from Turkey in the region. Israel has incurred severe economic damage as a result of being forced to fight this war. I believe that by providing Israel with the loan guarantees and thereby enabling Israel's economy to grow, the US will be advancing its own interest."

He continued, "As a fellow democracy that shares our values, that is fighting a war against terrorism, Israel is a friend, a strategic asset, and an ally for the US. A strong Israel is essential for advancing the US interest of building a stable world." Given this impassioned rhetoric, it is nearly impossible to imagine that Dean would have ceased to support the US's billion-dollar loan guarantees to Israel if he had been elected.

"The human rights situation in Israel and the Occupied Territories continues to deteriorate. Some 2,500 Palestinians, most of them unarmed and including some 450 children, have been killed by the Israeli army and more than 900 Israelis, most of them civilians and including more than 100 children, have been killed by Palestinian armed groups since the start of the current uprising, or intifada, in September 2000," contends Amnesty International. "Tens of thousand of Palestinians and thousands of Israelis have been injured, many maimed for life. Palestinians do not feel safe, in either the street or in their homes, as Israeli army aircrafts, helicopter gunships and tanks frequently shell Palestinian refugee camps and densely populated residential areas. Israelis also do not feel safe when they leave their homes, as Palestinian armed groups deliberately target Israeli civilians in suicide bombings and other attacks on buses, restaurants and other public places."

"In addition, Palestinians living under Israeli military occupation in the West Bank and Gaza Strip are subject to a wide range of human rights violations," the organization contends.

"Close to 20,000 Palestinians have been made homeless and thousands of others have lost their livelihood as the Israeli army has destroyed some 3,000 homes, vast areas of agricultural land and hundreds of other properties in the past three and a half years alone. Thousands of other houses have been damaged, many beyond repair. Israel's justification for the destruction is 'military/security necessity.' In Israel and in the East Jerusalem area security forces have also destroyed hundreds of homes of Palestinian citizens and residents of Israel on the grounds of lack of building permits."

When he was interviewed in *The Forward* in the fall 2002, Dean admitted that his position on Israel was "closer to AIPAC's" than that of Palestinian advocates, such as the Jewish-led Peace Now, and declared his support for building the wall that will separate Palestinians from their homeland.

Debunking the ignorance of the Israeli wall, Bernard Avishai, author of *The Tragedy of Zionism*, wrote in *Harper's* January 2005 issue:

> This is where the demographic argument gets you. You put West Bank Palestinians behind a wall where economic life is virtually impossible, and you hive off another hundred thousand Arab Israelis and put them behind the wall, too. Meanwhile, you expand your border to include non-Jewish settlements and maintain existing political economic barriers for Arab Israelis, a barrier of institutional practice and law, a barrier of land and common ideology. You say Jews and Arabs must be separated because even if Israel's Arab citizens will make the most of what liberties Israel gives them, they could not possibly want to be absorbed into Israel. And after all of this, you suppose yourself a democracy because you represent the general will of the "Jewish majority." But is the choice really Apartheid or binationalism?

In the aforementioned *Forward* issue Dean also championed

Israel for taking its battles across the border into Syria. "If Israel has to defend itself by striking terrorists elsewhere, it's going to have to do that," Dean told Judy Woodruff in a CNN interview. He followed this statement by claiming: "[T]errorism has no place in bringing peace in the Middle East … nations have the right to defend themselves just as we defended ourselves by going into Afghanistan to get rid of Al Qaeda."

Writer and journalist Robert Fisk argued in the UK's *Independent* on October 7, 2003, that Israel's attack was a lethal step toward a full-blown war in the Middle East:

> Yesterday, we took another little lethal step along the road to Middle East war, establishing facts on the ground, proving that it's permissible to bomb the territory of Syria in the "war against terror," which President Bush has himself declared now includes Gaza.
>
> And the precedents are there if we need them. Back in 1983, when President Reagan thought he was fighting a "war on terror" in the Middle East, he ordered his air force to bomb the Syrian army in the Lebanese Bekaa Valley, losing a pilot and allowing the Syrians to capture his co-pilot, who was only returned after a prolonged and politically embarrassing negotiation by Jesse Jackson. In an era when America is ready to threaten the invasion of Syria and Iran—part of that infamous "axis of evil"—this may seem small beer. But Syria itself has seen what has happened to America's army in Iraq, and is emboldened by its humiliation to avenge the attacks of Israel or America, whatever the cost.

Later, when Joseph Lieberman and Kerry questioned Dean's half-baked call for "peace" in Palestine, the former governor responded, "I was a little surprised because people who know me know very well I am a strong defender of Israel … But after I thought about it for a while, I wasn't surprised. I think that the connection of the Jewish community to Israel is so strong, and the feeling in Israel that someday they may be abandoned is enormous." Dean's own campaign website even went as far as to boast that the United States should "maintain its historic special relationship with the state of Israel, providing a guarantee of its long-term defense and security." Forget Palestine.

Defense and Iraq Reconstruction: Let the Bidding Begin

More recently, Howard Dean openly supported Bush's inflated Pentagon budget. With the 2004 cycle currently ringing in at $401.7 billion, Bush hopes to increase the military's budget to a staggering $500 billion by the end of the decade.

During a panel discussion in the summer 2003, Dean said that he didn't "agree with Dennis [Kucinich] about cutting the Pentagon budget when we're in the middle of a difficulty with terror attacks." And with keen bravado, Dean boasted that America's "superb military" is the essential deterrent against future terror attacks. What Dean did not understand was that defeating terrorists via military might is unlikely to stop terrorism, or halt the breeding of hatred toward the US in the Middle East.

Despite sounding like President Bush and company, it is worth noting a couple of items. First, Dean continually avoided criticizing President Clinton's efforts to expand the defense budget by $125 billion in the mid-1990s, which was the largest increase since the high-riding Reagan era.

Dean is, in essence, a hawk, not unlike Ronald Reagan. That Dean now represents the progressive wing of the Democratic Party shows how far right the pendulum of our national politics has swung. And this is exactly why Dean and the Democrat's political philosophy helped reelect Bush: the differences were so minimal, voters couldn't distinguish much variation, and consequently they stuck with what they knew.

As noted earlier, Dean also wholeheartedly supported

Bush's request for American taxpayers to fund the $87 billion "reconstruction" of Iraq. While it is well known that politically connected companies make out like bandits during wartime, Dean was not alarmed that this enormous sum of money was simply special-interest handouts for corporations seeking a stake in Iraq's future—oil.

Vice President Dick Cheney's Halliburton has by far been the largest beneficiary of the reconstruction funds. The company alone got $3.9 billion in 2003 to repair oil fields and provide laundry, food, sanitation and transportation services to the armed forces in Iraq.

How did Halliburton spend the dough? Reporting for Alternet.org on August 23, 2004, Pratap Chatterjee wrote:

> Whistle-blowers from the company have sent testimony to Congress detailing the many wasteful practices: paying $100 for a bag of laundry; abandoning $85,000 trucks for the lack of a spare tire. Meanwhile, other companies like Science Applications International Corporation of San Diego were shipping armored Humvees for company executives on specially chartered jets and paying themselves $200 an hour to run a [US] propaganda television station that no one was watching.
>
> An internal Pentagon audit completed two weeks ago and reported in the Wall Street Journal earlier this month found that Halliburton failed to adequately account for "more than $1.8 billion" it has received so far for providing logistical support to troops in Iraq and Kuwait.

Sure, Dean talked tough from time to time during his campaign about corporate authority over our government's policies. "The oil companies write our energy policy; big pharmaceutical companies draft Medicare reform without price controls," he trumped in November 2003. "And in Iraq, Halliburton is awarded a $1.7 billion no-bid contract." But since Dean made that statement, voters heard little from the Dean camp on Halliburton and other profiteers of the Iraq War. Could Dean have had ulterior motives for maintaining his silence?

You bet.

According to Federal Elections Commission records, Robert L. Crandall, former CEO of American Airlines, had given Dean $2,000 as of November 2003. It just so happens that Crandall has also been a member of the board of Halliburton since 1986.

While this individual donation didn't wed Dean to Cheney's Halliburton, monetary contributions are rarely disinterested. Had he not deflated so rapidly, the Dean campaign might have received additional donations from contractors, employees, and wealthy board members of companies involved in the reconstruction of Iraq.

Dean, after all, wanted to open up bidding to more of these conniving business interests. According to his website, Dean supported "[a]warding reconstruction contracts in a transparent and open process, not just to Halliburton—but to the best US or foreign bidder." It seems evident, then, that Dean would have neither abandoned nor halted the profiteering of Iraq. Opponents of the reconstruction efforts in Iraq note that Iraqi-run companies receive little assistance as they attempt to rebuild their war-torn countryside. And given Dean's refusal to shake the foundation of US foreign policy, there is little reason to believe that this injustice would not have persisted under a Dean presidency.

Sure Iraq deserves reconstruction. Indeed, Iraqi citizens deserve reparations for an illegal invasion. But such tasks and monies should be administered and awarded through international legal bodies, not by the occupier with clear sights on the country's major resource, oil.

Nevertheless, it's worth mentioning that Dean had a "solution" to help Iraqis reconstruct their country. Or rather, he had a solution for the US to profit from Iraqi reconstruction. Again on his website Dean contended, "The UN's Oil-for-Food program should be transformed into an Oil-for-Recovery program, to pay part of the costs of reconstruction and transition." This sounds good—until we realize that Iraq is to pay for damage done by the US with money from its own resources, when it is the US that should be paying.

Even on its own terms, illegal by international standards, the US was entirely wrong to invade Iraq. As of this writing, all pretexts for invasion, from the supposed Saddam/Al Qaeda link to the weapons of mass destruction, have been proven false.

Who is to pay for the enormous damage and loss of life for this folly? Far from arguing that the US should pick up the bill, Dean instead suggested Iraqis pay for our brutality. And that doesn't even address the damage done before the war when US backed UN sanctions crippled the country. Even as early as 1991, the UN had acknowledged that sanctions were causing the Iraqi people indisputable suffering and proposed a humanitarian program to alleviate malnutrition and disease.

Citing information on maternal and mortality rates collected by UNICEF, Professor Richard Garfield, in a report titled *Morbidity and Mortality Among Iraqi Children From 1990 to 1998: Assessing the Impact of Economic Sanctions,* which was commissioned by the Fourth Freedom Forum and the Joan B. Kroc Institute for International Peace Studies at the University of Notre Dame in 1998, estimated that between 1991 and 2002, the number of excess deaths among children under age five was 343,900 to 525,400.

Long before the campaign season and Dean's articulation of his position, it was well known, thanks to the information provided by UNICEF, that the dozen years of brutal sanctions imposed by the United Nations during the first Bush administration and Clinton's tenure killed thousands of innocent children and elderly people in Iraq. Yet Dean admitted he thought the Iraqis should pay for US transgressions.

Saddam Hussein, "We Got Him"

However, as Howard Dean repeatedly slipped and failed to radically challenge the tenets of Washington foreign policy, his comments regarding the US capture of the bearded Saddam were right on the mark.

Firing up his Democratic opponents and the White House on December 15, 2003, Dean told the Pacific Council of International Policy: "The capture of Saddam has not made America safer. The difficulties and tragedies we have faced in Iraq show the administration launched the war in the wrong way, at the wrong time, with inadequate planning, insufficient help, and at extraordinary costs."

However, it should not go unnoticed that even as Dean warned Saddam's fall would not make the US any safer, he vowed to continue fighting the war on terrorism Bush-style: call it shoot-from-the-hip diplomacy.

When Dean's opponents responded spitefully to the former governor's statement, few raised qualms. Senator Joseph Lieberman, likely a bit peeved about his old pal Al Gore's drooling endorsement of Howard Dean days earlier, exclaimed on December 16, 2003, that Dean was in a "spider-hole of denial," Insisting that "Saddam Hussein is a homicidal maniac, brutal dictator, supporter of terrorism and enemy of the United States, and there should be no doubt that America and the world are safer with him captured."

Lieberman was correct that Saddam was a maniac, and it is arguably true that Iraqis might have been safer without him had he been removed by an international force rather than one that became an occupier. But Lieberman's logic neglected to address the reality of what Iraqi faction would take over the country, as well as the internal violent dynamics that could have been present as opposing blocs sought power. But Dean's point was about America's safety, not Iraq's, and he was surely correct that Saddam Hussein's removal had no positive impact on terrorism in the US.

That same day, a reluctant supporter of Bush's war, John Kerry, remarked that Dean's "speech is still more proof that all the advisers in the world can't give Howard Dean the military and foreign policy experience, leadership skills, or diplomatic temperament necessary to lead this country through dangerous times."

Given that the Democrats lacked a coherent platform in their feeble attempts to disarm President Bush prior to Kerry's nomination, none of these remarks came as a surprise. But they might have been the death knell of the Democrats in the election to come.

As veteran White House correspondent Helen Thomas remarked in *The Seattle-Post Intelligencer* in early January 2004, "I have never seen so much antagonism directed at a candidate by other members of the same party. It seems to me his competitors would do better to toot their own horns instead of tearing down a colleague." She went on to add, "If they keep stomping on Dean, where will they be if he just happens to win the No. 1 spot on the ticket? Surely their words will come back to haunt them if they don't cop the nomination themselves. President Bush and his chief political guru will be laughing all the way to the polls. They already have enough fodder now for their campaign stops for the next 10 months."

This stomping fed an interesting dynamic: it helped paint Dean as an outsider, someone with clearly different priorities from the other candidates. Yet, as has been shown above, on Israel, on the war against Iraq, and on many other issues, the differences he had with other candidates hardly constituted a radical break from the unwritten platform of the Democratic Party, which, like their

Republican opposition, maintains undaunted support for military intervention around the globe. The attacks by Kerry, Lieberman, and others merely magnified the differences while obscuring the far more important similarities.

Despite the discord among the Democrats, Dean stood strong, turning himself into a self-proclaimed leader of the angry wing of the Democratic Party. Fittingly, Dean's observations about Saddam's capture at that December 15 event were far removed from those of a peacenik Vermonter.

On cue, pious Bush countered with a timely homily: "I believe, firmly believe—and you've heard me say this a lot, and I say it a lot because I truly believe it—that freedom is the almighty God's gift to every person—every man and woman who lives in this world. That's what I believe. And the arrest of Saddam Hussein changed the equation in Iraq. Justice was being delivered to a man who defied that gift from the Almighty to the people of Iraq."

It's no secret that Republicans hoped Saddam's capture would serve as a problem for the Democrat's disheveled foreign policy platform—and make Kerry's opposition mute on Election Day. As the Republicans learned prior to the 2002 congressional elections when they forced the Democrats to support the war resolution and then toppled Democratic control of the Senate, a broken opposition is no opposition at all. With this lesson in mind and Saddam in shackles, neo-cons knocked the wind right out of Dean and sucker-punched the rest of the Democrats on the issue of Iraq.

Iraq and the United Nations: Dean Waffles

Dean may have half-heartedly challenged Bush's unilateral Iraq war, but he didn't have a clue about how to end the occupation, and many critics failed to recognize that President Dean would not

have altered the nature of US involvement in the Middle East—
particularly in colonial Iraq.

As Dean stated in a primary debate in New Mexico on
September 4, 2003, "We cannot do this by ourselves. We have to
have a reconstruction of Iraq with the United Nations, with NATO,
and preferably with Muslim troops, particularly Arabic-speaking
troops from our allies such as Egypt and Morocco. We cannot
have American troops serving under UN command. We have
never done that before. But we can have American troops serving
under American command, and it's very clear to me that in order
to get the UN and NATO into Iraq, this President is going to have
to go back to the very people he humiliated, our allies, on the way
into Iraq, and hope that that they will now agree with us that we
need their help there. We were wrong to go in without the United
Nations, now we need their help, and that's not a surprise."

Noting Dean's assumption that the UN provides the answers
for Iraq, columnist Alexander Cockburn rebuked on December 4,
2003:

> Howard Dean has built his candidacy on clarion calls
> for the UN's supposedly legitimizing assistance in Iraq.
> Despite the political history of the Nineties many leftists
> still have a tendency to invoke the UN as a countervailing
> power. When all other argument fails, they fall back on
> the International Criminal Court, an outfit that should by
> all rights should have the same credibility as a beneficial
> institution as the World Bank or Interpol ... Another way of
> assaying the UN's role in Iraq is to remember that it made a
> profit out of its own blockade and the consequent starvation
> of hundreds of thousands of Iraqi babies in the 1990s. As a
> fee for its part in administering the oil-for-food program, the
> UN helped itself to 2 per cent off the top. (On more than one
> account members of the UN-approved Governing Council,
> whose most conspicuous emblem is the bank-looter Ahmad
> Chalabi, are demanding a far heftier skim in the present

looting of Iraq's national assets.) …

So what's the answer for Iraq? It doesn't take a genius to realize that more allied forces in Iraq will not expedite the so-called "transition period." As the guerilla street warfare in Iraq demonstrates, even after "elections," occupation is a hindrance—rather than a solution—to genuine democracy.

And as Tariq Ali, scholar and author of *Bush in Babylon: the Recolonialization of Iraq*, pointed out in a 2003 radio debate with a perplexed Christopher Hitchens on Amy Goodman's *Democracy Now!:* "You cannot have democracy without elections … What they will be faced with is the problem of constituent assembly, whoever is in a majority. They will unite on demanding a rapid end to the occupation, Iraqi control of Iraqi oil, and probably no military bases in Iraq. Which US administration is going to accept that?"

Certainly not Howard Dean's—for he too believed there were limits to what democracy should permit in Iraq. And like President Bush, Dean would not have tolerated the emergence of an Iraqi government that didn't befriend Israel or align itself with US interests.

Chapter Four

Business in Dean's World

Another Republican in Drag

"The joke among a lot of Vermont Republicans was
that they didn't need to run anyone for governor because they
basically had one in office already," said Harlan Sylvester, a
conservative Democratic stockbroker and longtime adviser
to Dean.

(St. Petersburg Times, July 6, 2003)

As Howard Dean planned his race for the White House, he
must have thumbed through George W. Bush's campaign
playbook. Within the first four months of Dean's announcement
of his bid for the White House, he had amassed over $110,000
in donations from people with ties to the Fund for a Healthy
America, a Vermont utility group. No, it's not Enron, but it's still
dirty money, if only because of the conflict of interest.

On February 27, 2002, David Gram of the Associated
Press reported: "One donor who gave Dean's PAC the maximum
amount allowed—$5,000 ... is Robert Young ... a top official at
two utility companies that have had a lot of important business
before state government during Dean's nearly 11 years in office.
Young is chief executive at Central Vermont Public Service Corp.
and chairman of Vermont Yankee Nuclear Power Corp."

Although Dean's campaign spokesperson Kate O'Conner
said it would be absurd for anybody to think donations to the
Dean campaign bought access, Dean seemed to believe otherwise.
"People who think they're going to buy a contract ... are mistaken,"
he stated in 1996 during the campaign reform bill debates. "But
they do get access—there's no question about that ... They get me

to return their phone calls."

Dean's distinction allows him to maintain a veneer of integrity: he claimed he was not for sale. But if such calls buy access, they buy the ability to help define the framework within which decisions are made, a framework that operates in the interests of industry, if not the outright interests of the individual firm from which the contribution comes.

And indeed they did. As Gram wrote, during Dean's transition into the governor's mansion, he called on utility executives to help with the change of office. It's no coincidence that those executives' businesses benefited greatly. Notes Gram:

* After years of pushing for the companies to absorb the excess costs of their expensive contract with Hydro-Quebec, Dean's Department of Public Service agreed to let ratepayers be billed for more than 90 percent of what those excess costs are expected to be in the coming years. The extra costs will be in the hundreds of millions of dollars.

* The department also agreed to allow the utilities to sell Vermont Yankee to a Pennsylvania company for a price that was expected to be $23.8 million by the time the deal closed. Shortly before the Public Service Board was to make a final decision on that sale, another company stepped in and offered more than seven times as much. That sale to Entergy Nuclear Corp. is currently before the board.

* After it became clear in the late 1990s that selling Vermont Yankee was a top goal of the utilities, the administration failed to heed warnings for more than two years that the money the nuclear plant was paying for emergency planning was much less than was needed. An administration official said there was concern about interfering with the sale.

So, Dean's administration in Vermont went along with the sale despite the burden placed on taxpayers. Dean also allowed Vermont Yankee to be sold to an out of state corporation, even though it was not likely to benefit Vermont residents, only the executives of the corporation that got Dean to return their phone calls.

When it comes to the matter of campaign contributors, James Dumont, a lawyer for the New England Coalition on Nuclear Pollution, seems to have hit the nail on the head, contending: "The [Dean Administration] didn't bite the hand that fed them."

Campaign Finance Farce

Most Americans, not just progressives, favor campaign finance reform and regulation, understanding instinctively that money can warp democracy. Thus, the positions of politicians on this issue reveal a great deal about how progressive they are and what their "liberalism" really represents.

Before his tenure ended in 2002, Dean proposed the gutting of Vermont's public financing statues. Advocates of the 1997 law claimed that the clauses Dean sought to destroy allowed individuals with minimal resources to run for public office and have any hope of winning.

As the Vermont Public Interest Research Group (VPIRG) responded to Dean's efforts:

> The Governor's move will simply open another door for access by corporations and other wealthy donors seeking generous tax breaks, permission to pollute our air and water, boondoggle electric rate contracts and other special interest perks ... Specifically, the law allows qualified candidates, regardless of political party affiliation, to run for governor or lieutenant governor using only clean, public dollars. The funding comes from voluntary contributions and corporate

fees.

Given these trends, it should come as no surprise that a 2003 report by the California-based Campaign Disclosure Project gave Dean's Vermont, which ranked 40th in the nation in campaign disclosure transparency, a failing grade.

"Vermont has much room to improve its efforts to make campaign finance information accessible to the public," the report claimed. "With a ranking in the bottom 10 states, Vermont has significant room to improve its campaign finance disclosure program."

A Rockefeller Republican

As governor, Dean was renowned for cutting state budgets and promoting rigid fiscal conservatism, which caused few Vermonters to consider Dean a friend of labor and blue-collar unions. IBM, one of Vermont's largest employers, consistently downsized its workforce as employees attempted to unionize. In August 2001, *Business Week* quoted the manager of government relations at IBM, in their Essex, Vermont plant as saying, "[Dean's] secretary of commerce would call me once a week just to see how things were going." But Dean rarely listened to labor advocates' concerns. And conservative pro-business Vermonters loved Dean's business agenda.

As *Business Week* reported, Wayne Roberts, a former Reagan official, considered Dean a "frugal man." Roger's blasted, "There is no way in heck he would tolerate a deficit." Vermont is not legally bound to balance the state's budget, but to Dean, it may as well have been.

In fact, on August 30, 2003, *The Washington Post* quoted former democratic president of the Vermont legislature and State Representative Dick McCormack as saying, "[Dean] made us very disciplined about spending, even if we didn't really like it. I was a liberal Democrat, and I fought him a lot."

John McClaughry, president of the Ethan Allen Institute, a conservative Vermont think-tank, says, "The Howard Dean you are seeing on the national scene is not the Dean that we saw around here for the last decade." Dean's evolving rhetoric, say his critics, can be attributed to his political ambitions and the need to rally his youthful supporters.

But despite his oratory shift, Dean, who boasted about balancing Vermont's budget, was still an old school banker at heart.

"I'm a fiscal conservative," Dean said early in his campaign. "I'm most proud of our fiscal stability—I left the state in better shape than I found it … Capitalism is a great system."

There's nothing inherently wrong with fiscal conservatism, and a great deal can be said for a government living within its means. Like a household, wise fiscal policy can include saving money during good times, as a cushion to be spent to see a state or country through hard times. The issue is, where does one act frugally, cutting back on subsidies to private business, a bloated defense budget, or social services? Unfortunately, Dean's commitment to a balanced budget put the brunt of the cost on the public, particularly those struggling financially, while spending liberally on business needs. Dean's endorsement of former House Speaker Newt Gingrich's fiscal dexterity in the 1990s was grossly apparent. Repeatedly praising Gingrich for slashing Medicare and other social programs to help balance the federal budget, Dean said, "The way to balance the [federal] budget is for Congress to cut Social Security, move the retirement age to 70 … [cut] Medicare and veterans pensions, while the states cut everything else."

Dean, not surprisingly, took that initiative—and thousands of Vermonters suffered as a result. As the Associated Press reported on November 24, 2003, "[Dean cut] programs for the elderly, blind, and disabled when balancing budgets … [And he cut] some social programs in Vermont." In the name of "fiscal responsibility," Dean also gouged the Aid to Needy Families with Children program, public education, as well as funding for public defendants. In other words, he attacked those most in need, precisely the opposite of what progressivism is supposed to stand for.

A quick glance at the numbers puts Dean's politics in stark relief. In all, Dean cut $6 million in state education and retirement funds for public school teachers, $7 million in state employee benefits, $4 million in health care for the elderly, $2 million in welfare programs earmarked for the disabled and blind, and $1.2 million in Medicaid benefits. Dean, of course, deemed these cuts "mandatory" and "unavoidable" given Vermont's $60 million deficit.

But as Vermonter and activist Keith Rosenthal pointed out in the *International Socialist Review*, Dean footed the bill for a new $30 million prison in Springfield, Vermont, $7 million for a low-interest loan program for businesses, and cut the state's income tax—which accounted for about $30 million in revenue—by 8 percent. In fact, by 2002, Dean's prosecutor-friendly government increased investment in state prisons by nearly 150 percent, while funds for state colleges increased by a mere 7 percent.

Notice that no one maneuver is "unavoidable" to resolve a deficit: a government can increase taxes on wealthier segments, cut back on prison spending, and exercise a whole range of choices. Dean chose to stiff the disabled, the blind, and others in need.

Not surprisingly, many liberal Vermont state legislators, angered by Dean's balancing tactics, did not feel good about "cutting taxes in a way that benefits the wealthiest taxpayers."

But what is so wrong with singing the tune of balanced budget responsibility? As economist Robert Pollin of the University of Massachusetts at Amherst explains in his latest book, *Contours*

*of Descent: US Economic Fractures and the Landscape of Global
Austerity*:

> The first reason for the government to run deficits
> ... is that it is a powerful tool for counteracting recessions.
> During a recession, spending by households and businesses
> slumps. Businesses then respond to the overall fall in sales
> by laying off workers and otherwise reducing the scale of
> their operations. This rise in unemployment leads to further
> cuts in household and business spending. Government deficit
> spending is able to reverse this self-reinforcing slide toward
> deepening recession.
>
> The other major positive reason for governments to
> go into deficit is to finance expensive, long-term capital
> investments, in areas such as education, environmental
> protection, or public infrastructure because these long-term
> investments will yield higher productivity and other long-
> term benefits ... To assume that the federal government
> should never go into debt to finance a new school building is
> analogous to saying that a household should never take out a
> mortgage to purchase a home.

Pollin's point is instructive: deficit spending can be
productive. And the lesson of Dean is also enlightening: fiscal
conservatism can be destructive. The key to either policy is what
the money is spent on: meaningful investment that benefits large
numbers of people, or subsidies and tax breaks for those who
don't need them.

We might be tempted to see Bush and Dean as night and day
fiscally, given Bush's massive deficit, which rang in at $412 billion
in 2004. Yet Bush is trying to lower deficits by cutting back social
programs such as Social Security. Had Dean become president,
we might have seen a repeal of the tax breaks; however, based on
his record as governor, we may have seen Howard Dean wage a
massive war of social services—just like Bush.

Vermont as Little Bermuda

Keeping the capitalist spirit alive and kicking in Vermont, Dean's disregard for Medicare and other social programs certainly helped make the state attractive for corporate influx and takeover.

During his presidential campaign, Dean denounced certain corporations for setting up offshore accounts in order to avoid paying income tax: "It's time to look behind the fiction that allows corporations to become citizens of places like Bermuda and avoid paying income taxes on their foreign income," he said in an Associated Press article. In 2001, Dean went so far as to say that he wanted Vermont to "overtake Bermuda" as the "world's largest" haven for captive insurance companies. And he worked hard to make that a reality. As the *Boston Globe* reported on December 19, 2003:

> ... to attract companies to set up so-called 'captive' insurance businesses in Vermont, [Dean] signed legislation that enabled a Bermuda-based company to establish a Vermont branch, which industry analysts said at the time could provide a tax break for the parent firm ... In May 1999, Dean signed a bill designed to help self-owned, or 'captive,' insurance companies that intended to remain offshore. The legislation, for example, allowed an offshore-based captive insurance company to set up a 'branch' in Vermont as a way of complying with US labor laws. This occurred when the captive wanted to cover employee benefits, a new form of business for the captives. The branch was not in an actual building, but was an operation run by Vermont-based specialists in the insurance business.

Ironically, Enron, the fraudulent corporation Dean loved to criticize Bush for being connected to, profited greatly from Dean's 1999 tax-haven bill. By moving to Vermont, the Gulf Company, Ltd., the captive insurance company that Enron opened in Vermont, avoided paying millions in federal income taxes since

Dean gladly decreased premiums for such insurance companies to ensure that corrupt corporations moved in and set up shop. Enron, meanwhile, still owed millions of dollars to the Gulf Company upon going belly up in 2001.

DuPont Chemical, another corporate polluter that basked in the sunshine of Dean's little Bermuda, had its insurance premiums cut by over 60 percent in 1993 by Governor Dean. All the while Dean staunchly balanced the state budget and cut spending for much needed social programs. Gingrich would be proud.

Although Dean has not yet revealed whether he met with executives of these companies, Molly Lambert, Dean's Secretary of Commerce, noted: "[Dean would] meet personally with captive owners … they went to his office, or he went to them."

Trading in Vermont: The Neoliberal Spirit

Fully endorsing the free market, deregulation, and privatization while disregarding government oversight, Dean's heart sided with the neoliberal American ruling elite every step of the way.

As the Associated Press reported in November 1994, Dean supported the devastating Fast Track legislation, which allows trade agreements to move rapidly through Congress, so that they will not be picked apart for their flaws and potential downsides. Critics of Fast Track contend that these expedited actions end up being harmful for US workers and the environment, as they are pushed forward in an undemocratic way. The National Family Farm Coalition and the Western Association of Resource Councils argue that "Fast track [is] a detriment to family farmers, rural communities, and working people because it fails to meet the principles of a fair trade policy that promotes global food security while sustaining family farms and competitive markets."

"In the wake of the '94 midterm elections, Dean urged

moving full speed ahead on further trade agreements: [Colorado Gov.] Romer, Dean, and the third participant … said the governors urged Clinton to build on the bipartisan dealings he has had with congressional Republicans on trade issues … In that vein, they urged him to resist the advice of more liberal Democrats who are urging Clinton to adopt a confrontational approach. 'I can assure you there was no one at the table arguing the president should go to the left,' Dean said."

And in a letter that Governor Dean sent President Clinton in 1999, he urged the President to expand US trade with China, saying, "I completely agree with your assessment about the importance of this vote to national security and to the future of Sino-American relations long into the future … On the Democratic side … [we face] the enormous pressure which will be brought to bear by the labor movement during an election year."

A devout Clinton loyalist, Dean also supported the North American Free Trade Agreement (NAFTA), the International Monetary Fund (IMF), and the World Bank—and still defends all three. These policies and institutions, as will become clear below, cost American workers dearly. Nevertheless, anyone that saw Dean on the podium along the campaign trail might think otherwise given the rhetorical shift in his position on international trade.

Dean's move was likely a calculated one, intended to appease his grassroots base, which largely opposed free trade agreements backed by the United States. If he had been elected, Dean most certainly would not have pulled out of NAFTA or disregarded the IMF and the World Bank's abuse of power. Although he acknowledged NAFTA's failures, Dean has never second-guessed his support of the neoliberal policies of the Clinton 90s. "I supported NAFTA, I supported the WTO. We benefited in Vermont from trade," he claimed during a 2003 Democratic primary debate at Pace University. "My position on trade is pretty clear … however, the problem is that these trade agreements are skewed toward multinational corporations. They benefit them, but they do not have equal protection for the people who work either in this country or elsewhere."

What Dean never understood, many experts argue, is that such agreements were not negotiated with the rights of workers and the environment in mind—hence the loss of an estimated 775,000 US jobs since 1994, and an immeasurable impact on the natural environment. Because amendments to these statues cannot eliminate the muscle neoliberal policymakers have flexed throughout the last few decades, a Dean administration would have had a difficult—if not impossible—task of shifting the burden of free trade from workers and the environment to multinational corporations without abandoning such doctrine altogether.

"Had [the original promises] come true, NAFTA would have been an enormous boom, and we would all be cracking champagne," says Lori Wallach, director of the consumer rights group Public Citizen. "But instead we have got the 10-year record and it's pretty damn grim," adds Wallach. "NAFTA's 10-year record demonstrates that under the NAFTA model, most people in the three countries were losers, while only a few of the largest corporations who helped write NAFTA were the major winners."

But Dean believes that such free trade agreements are in the long-term interest of the United States. "I still think NAFTA was a good thing. But 10 years into NAFTA, we have shipped a lot of our industrial capacity to other countries," Dean admitted in an interview with Joe Klein on March 26, 2003. "The reason for NAFTA is not just trade. It's defense and foreign policy. A middle class country where women fully participate in the economic and political decision making of that country is a country that doesn't harbor groups like Al Qaeda, and it's a country that does not go to war. So that's why trade is really in our long-term interest. So far NAFTA has transferred industrial capacity, but we haven't transferred any of the elements that are needed to make a middle class. The trade union movement built America because they allowed people who worked in factories and mines to become middle class. America is the strongest country on earth because we have the largest middle class on earth, with democratic ideals. Working people in this country feel that this is their country, and they have a piece of the pie, and it matters what they think." Dean added, "I don't think my support of NAFTA 10 years ago was a bad thing."

But those young women Dean touts have never become "full participants" in the global economy because they have not benefited from neoliberal economics in real terms. And let us not forget the 750,000 middle class jobs that were lost during the 1990s boom. How will free trade ever bring them back?

However tantalizing Dean's rhetoric may have seemed to the dizzied Deaniacs, he still ignored the fact that free trade agreements have escalated the annihilation of a class of people here in the United States by transferring middle class jobs overseas and to Mexico, where monstrous multinationals race to the bottom to gobble up cheap labor forces. And contrary to Dean's claims (which he growled repeatedly while campaigning) about how much Vermont benefited from NAFTA, exports during his tenure declined by more than 38 percent, and Vermont's workforce lost jobs. According to a 2003 report by the Progressive Policy Institute, a research group for the Democrat's own Leadership Council, 6,123 jobs were lost in Vermont between 1994 and 2000, due to foreign trade.

And yet Dean stated if he had to vote again, he would still support NAFTA?

The pattern that emerges is one of great harm to Vermont's citizens. Dean backs policies that lose jobs. This no doubt contributes to a budget deficit because fewer jobs lower the tax base while raising the number of people who need public assistance. Dean then responds to this with fiscal conservatism at the expense of programs that might help people get back on their feet. Sadly, there is nothing remarkable about a politician pursuing such a cycle in the interests of serving the wealthy.

Chapter Five

In Vermont, the Prosecution Never Rests

Law According to the Doc

The poor weren't the only ones in need that were attacked by Howard Dean. As governor, Dean argued that the legal system unfairly benefited criminal defendants over prosecutors.

His antagonism toward legal defense was apparent, for instance, in his relationship with Robert Appel, Vermont's defender general. In 1999, Dean blocked Appel from accepting over $150,000 in federal grants, which were to provide legal representation for mentally ill defendants. Two years later, Dean elected not to reappoint the four-term defender general, whose ideology and interpretation of the law often clashed with Dean's. It didn't help that Appel openly aired his frustration with Dean's view of constitutional rights. When the governor suggested that defendants get all the breaks, Appel countered, "I would say it is a fundamental difference in perspective between me and my boss."

As Vermont's *Rutland Herald* suggested in a 2001 editorial regarding Dean's stonewall of the aforementioned funds,

> for Dean to block a government agency from receiving federal money was unusual in itself. But Dean's openly expressed bias against criminal defendants provided a partial explanation. Dean has made no secret of his belief that the justice system gives all the breaks to defendants. Consequently, during the 1990s, state's attorneys, police, and corrections all received budget increases vastly exceeding increases enjoyed by the defender general's office. That meant the state's attorneys were able to round up ever increasing numbers of criminal defendants, but the public defenders were not given comparable resources to respond.

The editorial went on to add that such funds are typically used to pay for expert testimony in criminal cases. Because such resources are imperative to guaranteeing the right to a fair trial for mentally disabled defendants, it should be evident that Dean didn't just oppose justice for defendants. He undermined it.

What is intriguing here are the implications of Dean's position for justice. In this instance he wasn't taking a "get tough" stance on criminals, on people who had been proven guilty. Rather, he was blocking federal funds to defendants, people who, for the most part, had not yet been proven guilty. Cutting off resources to those who are, according to the famous phrase, "innocent until proven guilty" amounts to blocking justice, and has nothing to do with a penchant for law and order that is so popular with voters these days. Indeed, Dean's stance, to the extent it prevents people exercising their rights and defending themselves, is antithetical to law and order.

Supreme Choices; Moving Toward 16th Century Justice

When Bob Kinzel of the Vermont News Service interviewed Dean in July 1997, the Governor boasted, "I'm looking to steer the [Vermont Supreme C]ourt back towards consideration of the rights of the victims."

Dean also told Kinzel that he sought to expedite the judicial process and appoint state judges who were willing to undermine the Bill of Rights.

Governor Dean claimed he was "looking for someone who is for justice" and believed such justices should "quickly convict guilty criminals." According to Dean, the judicial system "does not emphasize truth and justice over lawyering. It emphasizes legal technicalities and rights of the defendants, and all that …"

Believing that constitutional protections—or what Dean termed "legal technicalities"—undermine speedy trials, he sought judges who deemed "common sense more important than legal technicalities."

But as Leighton Detora, president of the Vermont Trial Lawyers Association, told the Vermont Press Bureau on July 17, 1997: "I don't think [Dean] has any regard for any process that gets in the way of what he wants to accomplish ... he was trying to move the justices around like chess pieces there. He's a doctor, and as such, he has all the learned responses to the legal profession—that we are just out here, and lawyers' jobs are to make things more complicated. In his own arrogance, I think he somehow thinks he has a lock on truth and wisdom."

The Governor's Constitutional Hang-Up

Shortly after the September 11, 2001 attacks, Dean told David Gram of the Associated Press that the United States needs to "[reevaluate] the importance of some ... civil liberties."

When asked if he thought the Bill of Rights needed to be amended, Dean answered, "I think it is unlikely, but I frankly haven't gotten that far."

Although Dean certainly wasn't the only politician making such comments following this horrific event, the fact that his reaction failed to distinguish him from the rest of the mainstream political field is a good indicator of how Dean might have responded following the gruesome attacks had he been president.

To Dean's credit, he did call for the mysterious Patriot Act II to be halted. But given his reactions to the terrorist attacks on September 11 and his broader disregard for constitutional law, it is difficult to imagine that President Dean would not have supported these draconian laws when pressured by civil rights attackers.

Dean's disregard for the necessity of upholding constitutional guarantees following the terrorist attacks in 2001 is unfortunately symptomatic of his widespread lack of concern for justice and liberty. When Tim Russert asked Dean about his support for the death penalty on *Meet the Press* in June of 2003, the Governor replied:

"The problem with life without parole is that people get out for reasons that have nothing to do with justice. We had a case where a guy who was a rapist, a serial sex offender, was convicted, then was let out on what I would think and believe was a technicality, a new trial was ordered and the victim wouldn't come back and go through the second trial."

For Dean, a "technicality" seems to be synonymous with "constitutional hang-up." In the case Dean presented to Russert, the Governor believed a man walked free when he should have been put to death rather than exercising his right to challenge his unconstitutional conviction. As *Washington Post* columnist Richard Cohen commented:

> In all my years writing about the death penalty, I have never heard any politician admit that he would countenance the death of an innocent person in order to ensure that the guilty die. Dean is maybe the first to acknowledge the unacknowledgeable. For that, I suppose, he ought to be congratulated. But by equating the murder of one individual by another with the murder of an innocent person by the government—the unpreventable with the preventable— he has casually trashed several hundred years of legal safeguards.

However, when it came to the question of international law, Dean called for a fair trial of both Saddam Hussein and the cave-dwelling Osama bin Laden. But in the broader context of Dean's notion of justice and "fair" trials, one cannot honestly deem the doctor a human rights advocate or a progressive proponent of criminal justice reform.

Judicial Watch vs. Howard

Dean's disregard for the rule of law goes well beyond what he believes is best for the system. For Dean, who was accused of preventing public access to his gubernatorial records, lawbreaking is also a personal affair.

According to an October 2003 statement by Judicial Watch, a group that is nonpartisan in its litigation, Vermont archivist Greg Sanford sent an official letter to the Vermont Governor's Council in 2002, when the governor's office was pressing to seal all records as Dean set his sights on the White House. As Sanford noted in his letter, "ambition" was not a sufficient reason to block access to government documents since Vermont's open record laws (V.S.A. § 315) clearly oppose such actions.

As the law states, "It is in the public interest to enable any person to review and criticize [the officers' of the government] decisions even though such examination may cause inconvenience and embarrassment."

On this account, Judicial Watch sued the former governor of Vermont on December 3, 2003, and demanded the release of more than 146 boxes and 400,000 pages of concealed records.

During a Democratic presidential debate on January 4, 2003, Dean insisted, "We have turned everything over to the attorney general of the state of Vermont. And the attorney general of the state of Vermont will go to court, and a judge will look over every document in our records. And they are free to release whatever they'd like ..." He also explained, "[A]mong these records is a group of letters from people who wrote me during the civil unions crisis, or the civil unions bill-passing, which was a crisis in Vermont because it was the most contentious bill that we had for many, many years." But this cannot possibly explain all 140-plus boxes, particularly since Vermont Attorney General Sorrell—who believed Dean's concealed records were not subject to Vermont's record law—tried to block access to these records.

"Judicial Watch, Inc. is not presently entitled to inspect the gubernatorial papers that were sealed by Governor Dean," wrote Sorrell, who later announced, "We think we've got a strong case here. The Vermont Supreme Court has repeatedly acknowledged the validity of executive privilege." But while the Vermont Supreme Court may have acknowledged this, state law never has.

On the day of the Wisconsin Democratic primaries, a Vermont court ruled against Dean. According to a posting on Judicial Watch's website immediately following the ruling, "The state court ruled today that a private agreement between Dean and the State of Vermont could not be used to prevent public access to Dean's records." Unfortunately, the blocking and unblocking of the documents mattered little for Dean, who endured two loses on the same chilly February day—one at the Wisconsin polls and another in an old Vermont courtroom.

Meetings on the Hush-Hush

Early in his campaign Dean suggested the Bush "administration should level with the American people about just how much influence Ken Lay and his industry buddies had over the development of the president's energy policy by releasing notes on the deliberations of Vice President Cheney's energy task force."

How could Dean criticize Bush's faults on this matter when he never came clean himself? As the Associated Press reported on December 28, 2003, Dean's Vermont Energy Group frequently met privately. The article contended:

> Dean's group held one public hearing and after-the-fact volunteered the names of industry executives and liberal advocates it consulted in private, but the Vermont governor refused to open the task force's closed-door deliberations …

In 1998, Dean's Vermont task force met in secret to write a plan for revamping state electricity markets ... Elizabeth Bankowski, who served as the other co-chair of the task force, told the legislature that the requirement the task force meet in secret 'was decided in advance by the governor's office and the governor's lawyer.' Dean's lawyer argued the secrecy was permitted under a 1988 legal change.

As Detora suggested, Dean, like Bush, seemed to believe he had a lock on "truth and wisdom."

Chapter Six

Developing Vermont

The Governor's Environmental Record

W hile he chummed up with Enron execs and other white-collar criminals, Dean hobnobbed with big-time developers as well, hoping that their corporations would decorate Vermont with the destructive enmities of suburban America. And the cold Governor got his wish to preserve the model of "support expansion, no matter how it affects the environment" that President Bill Clinton made illustriously famous.

As Ron Jacobs, Vermont community activist and author of *The Way the Wind Blew: a History of the Weather Underground*, recalls, "Despite the fact that Vermont has relatively tough laws regarding the pace and breadth of development, Dean's tenure saw the expansion of industry and strip development at a rate much greater than his predecessors. While some of this may have been unavoidable given the devastating reach of global capitalism, Dean was often actively involved in encouraging these corporations to set up shop in Vermont—supporting tax breaks and allowing them to ignore/avoid key steps in the environmental impact review process. Whether the issue was power and cellular lines across mountaintops, gas pipelines through forests, or pesticide use by factory farms, Dean's policies were too often on the side of those who prefer profits over environmental protection."

He continued, "During Dean's tenure … it seemed like there was no business that he didn't like, nor any program existing for poor people that he wouldn't cut to keep his budget balanced."

"Dean wasn't standing up for sustainable development. During his watch, we saw a lot more sprawl and strip development. Instead of telling the developer[s] to build in an industrial park, he showed them a green field and allowed them to build in a green field," said Mark Sinclair, a Vermont attorney with the Conservation Law Foundation.

"Convert farm fields into pavement. Once again, when there was a conflict between sprawl and big development, Governor Dean sided with big development. He doesn't believe in land use planning, and provided no funding for Vermont's towns to do the planning they need," Sinclair added. "As a result, Vermont reacts to development. The only reason we don't look like Maryland is because we are a colder climate and people are just discovering us."

According to Michael Colby, another Vermont resident and environmental activist, Dean's promotion of so-called sustainable development failed Vermont's environment.

As Colby wrote in *Wild Matters* in February 2002: "Remember, when Dean took office, there were no Wal-Marts in Vermont; there were no Home Depots; Burlington's downtown was dominated by local stores not the national chains that now rule the roost; there were 36% more small farmers in existence; there were no 100,000-hen mega-farms; and sprawl wasn't a word on the tip of everyone's tongue.

"Interestingly, Dean told the *Burlington Free Press* in early 2004 that he wished the rest of 'the country were more like Vermont.' But it certainly seems Dean has been doing his best to make Vermont more like the rest of the country."

Annette Smith, director of Vermonters for a Clean Environment, emphasized, "EP under Governor Dean meant Expedite Permits, not Environmental Protection ... Dean's attempt to run for president as an environmentalist is nothing but a fraud. He's destroyed the Agency of Natural Resources, he's refused to meet with environmentalists while constantly meeting with the development community, and he's made the permitting process one big dysfunctional joke."

Stephanie Kaplan, former executive of Vermont's Environmental Board and Vermont environmental lawyer, was quoted by Colby as saying, "Under Dean the Act 250 process (Vermont's primary development review law) and the Agency of Natural Resources (ANR) have lost their way. Dean created the myth that environmental laws hurt the economy and set the tone to allow Act 250 and the ANR to simply be permit mills for developers," explained Kaplan. "After the post-C&S purge the burden of proof for Act 250 permits switched from being on the applicants—where it's supposed to be—to being on the environmentalists. That's why 98% of the permit requests are approved and only 20% ever have hearings."

Dean's Smokescreens: Hot Coals in Vermont

Dean's fancy for development wasn't his only enviro-absurdity. While Dean often talked tough about environmental protection and expanding renewable energy sources, his record conveyed quite a different story—a tale that was so anti-environmental that Dean never received the endorsement of the prominent Sierra Club in any of his five gubernatorial campaigns—this despite the Sierra Club being a pro-corporate environmental organization.

When California's energy crisis peaked, Dean was debating whether to build a coal-fired plant in Vermont. Although Dean required car dealerships to sell a certain number of electric cars per year, he was never mistaken for an environmentalist, let alone a conservationist.

As Jonathan Lesser wrote in the *Burlington Free Press* following the proposed coal plant incident, "The resulting hue and cry [by environmentalists] was so strident that [Dean] might as well have proposed a state holiday celebrating child molesters."

In neighboring downwind New Hampshire, observers,

including Steve Blackledge, director of New Hampshire Public Interest Research Group, described Dean's coal vision as "clearly the wrong approach." "Coal plants pollute more than other fossil fuels," explained Blackledge. "And if Governor Dean wants diversity in fuel source, he should be pushing clean renewables."

"I'm a little surprised and distressed to learn that the governor of Vermont seems to think that a new direction in Vermont's energy policy requires more coal-fired power plants, given what we know about the contribution coal-fired plants to air pollution," said Charles Niebling, who worked for the Society for the Preservation of New Hampshire Forests at the time.

These observers weren't alone in their criticism of Dean. In fact, criticism of his proposal was so widespread that Dean had no choice but to back off, lest he commit political suicide.

In Defense of Polluters; Agricultural Crisis in Vermont

A repeat defender of dangerous levels of pesticide use on Vermont farms, Dean invariably took heat from the lively environmental group Vermonters for a Clean Environment.

In 1999, Vermont resident Judy Ferraro wrote the governor's office complaining about pesticide poisoning from her neighboring orchard farm. As Ferraro explained, "Our gravest concern is that we are being exposed to these toxic chemicals in the air we breathe; inhalation of pesticides is the most dangerous kind of exposure, and it is the most difficult to monitor. Many days I have called to my children to come indoors and shut the windows to protect ourselves. We have experienced burning eyes and lips when standing by our front door. Our property is surrounded on three sides by orchards … Last year, after many phone calls and pleas for assistance," Ferraro recalled, "the head of the Agriculture Department came to our place to check things out first hand. He was clearly disturbed by what he saw."

As a report by Vermonters for a Clean Environment noted, countless organized citizens wrote Dean, hoping to persuade him to intervene and prohibit the use of harmful chemicals on Vermont farms. One of the first Vermonters to speak out about the problem, Ashley Green (a pseudonym used in the report), has been writing to complain about her neighbor's pesticide use since early 1992.

In January 2001, Green wrote Governor Dean, saying of her neighbor, "The grower in this case is using some chemicals that are recognized carcinogens. Increasingly, research is showing links between chemical exposure and disease, and children are most vulnerable to the effects of chemicals. I am very concerned with the chemical exposure my two children are getting. Recently I learned of a study in the Netherlands that has documented mild cognitive dysfunction in people exposed to pesticides, including problems with numbers, letters, and speech. Both my children are now receiving special aid at school for speech difficulties. Is there a correlation? I don't know. But it seems that our current agricultural standards and Department of Agriculture permit land use practices that are potentially hazardous."

Dean all but ignored Vermonters' complaints, siding instead with the polluters. In an *Amicus* brief the state filed in October 2001, regarding another farm in Vermont, the defense claimed there was not "a substantial adverse effect on the public health and safety" and that the farm was "in compliance with Vermont's water quality standards."

This defense came after an Addison County Superior Court Judge found that the orchard was a "nuisance." According to the report, Vermont's Department of Agriculture, Food and Markets (DAFM) "repeated the history of the department's advice to move the pesticide mixing area in 1995 and again in 1996, noting that at the time of the violation in June 2001 'the mixing and loading area remained unchanged from the previous investigations.' The violation charged: 'The orchard worker mixed pesticides that resulted in either the pesticide product, dilution, or rinsate entering an unnamed stream, thus violating 6 VSA Section 1111(a)(6).'"

Even though the courts acknowledged the negative effects on small egg and dairy farmers, the lower courts argued that "pre-existence" of the polluting farms was a sufficient reason to allow corporate farms to continue conducting their practices. In late 2003, the Supreme Court of Vermont ruled that the legislature must decide on how to deal with these claims, but as of January 2004, the Vermont legislature had yet to follow suit.

Dean's lackluster farm policies forced native Vermonter John Tremblay to move his family to New Hampshire. During his move Tremblay contended in the Vermonters for a Clean Environment report that Dean "is a business man with big money. He is not a farmer. He doesn't care about the people or the environment. He doesn't care that the air stinks or that there are flies everywhere. He doesn't care that his trucks ruin the roads and make it unsafe for your children to ride their bikes. He doesn't care that he destroys your way of life, and unfortunately the state of Vermont doesn't care either."

Fran Bessette, a small Vermont dairy farmer who is also irate over Dean's polluter-friendly politics, notes that the DAFM allowed Canadian hog-growing multi-millionaire Lucien Breton to open up a huge polluting egg factory in Highgate, Vermont. Unfortunately, Bessette claims, small Vermont farmers have paid the price for Dean's disregard for environmental protections.

Bessette and her neighbors have been victims of a number of problems, including "flies, noise, odors, traffic, air quality, disease, chemical exposure, loss of property values, increased stress, and significant impacts on water." When Bessette voiced her concerns, Dean either ignored them altogether or was what Bessette termed "vicious" in his replies.

As Dean wrote in a response to Bessette, "As you know, Leon Graves, Commissioner of Agriculture, has said he will deny

Vermont Egg Farm a permit to expand until the fly problem has been taken care of." But Dean never said he was going to address Bessette's grievance or that he supported the plight of Vermont farmers against a Canadian hog-baron.

When Sherry Kawecki testified at the reconfirmation hearings for Vermont Agriculture Commissioner Leon Graves, Kawecki stated: "Commissioner of Agriculture Leon Graves has lost the respect of both farmers and the consumers of this state. By his actions, he has shown disdain for small farmers, thumbed his nose at laws set by the legislature and sold out to corporate special interests."

Despite this, Dean had the nerve to claim in an August 12, 2003 CNN interview that "The destruction of the middle class and the widening gap between the rich and poor is being played out right before our eyes, with the concentration of [power allocated to] the agriculture industry."

We are "victims in this nightmare," Bessette concluded. "Dean washed his hands [of] the whole ordeal. We suffered major impacts from all this. If [people] want the truth on how Dean handled this, tell them to ask the victims, us."

Chapter Seven

Comforting the Homefront with Hollow Answers

A Domestic Liability

"The reason I don't support legalization or decriminalization [of drugs] is because we already have enough trouble with the two drugs that are legal: tobacco and alcohol."

Howard Dean, Philadelphia Weekly, August 6, 2003

Howard Dean had a tough time during October 2003, when Democratic challenger Al Sharpton mounted an attack on what he called an anti-affirmative action, pro-death penalty, pro-gun agenda.

Shortly after Rev. Sharpton (who brought on GOP guru Roger Stone to orchestrate his campaign in its waning months) learned that Rep. Jesse Jackson, Jr., planned to endorse the former Vermont governor, he announced, "Dean's opposition to affirmative action, his current support for the death penalty and historic support of the NRA's agenda, amounts to an anti-black agenda." Sharpton concluded that "[Dean's positions] will not sell in communities of color."

Highlighting Dean's liability to communities of color, Sharpton cited a 1995 statement made on CNN's *Late Edition* by Dean, who said, "We ought to look at affirmative action programs based not on race, but on class, and opportunities to participate." Dean angrily responded to Sharpton's comment, insisting, "[My comment was] about help[ing] people who don't have any money, and I think we should do that. But I also think affirmative action has to be about race, and I've said that all throughout this campaign."

Savvy Sharpton responded, "If Dean has changed his position [on affirmative action], he should just say so, but don't accuse others of not talking straight." Because Dean didn't address Sharpton's other critiques, observers are left wondering where Dean really stands on gun rights and the death penalty—and why communities of color really did side with John Edwards and Sharpton during the early primaries in the South.

Government-Sponsored Death

As mentioned earlier, Dean, who admitted he would—as Richard Cohen put it—"countenance the death of an innocent person in order to ensure that the guilty die," has a perplexing penchant for the death penalty.

During the 1990s, Dean changed his position on the death penalty and shied away from his impassioned opposition of old. As Dean's official website explained: "When he became governor in 1991, Howard Dean opposed the death penalty in all cases. In 1997, after a number of brutal crimes involving the murder of children, including the abduction, rape, and murder of 12-year-old Polly Klass in California, Dean spoke publicly about his reconsideration of his position on the death penalty."

The defense babbled on: "After careful deliberation, Dean concluded that the death penalty may be an appropriate punishment in limited circumstances such as the murder of a child or a police officer. Finally, as a result of the mass murder that took place on September 11, 2001, he concluded that the death penalty should also be available in cases of terrorists who take human life."

Now supporting the death penalty, albeit only in certain circumstances, Dean seems to have aligned himself with President Bush, who is renowned for executing some 131 convicts during his tenure as governor of the Lone Star State. But while Bush too defends the death penalty in specific cases, Dean claims he doesn't support its application in as *many* instances as Bush Junior. Both, however, contend that they know best and have the moral authority to decide who should be salvaged or murdered by the State.

Moreover, Dean ignored the racist aspects of the United States' heinous tradition. As Dean supported the death penalty in extreme cases, he failed to address the disparate application of the death penalty to poor minority convicts. Any just critique of the federal death penalty would have acknowledged these egregious injustices.

After all, according to a study released by US Department of Justice (DOJ) in September 2000, poor blacks are disproportionately sentenced to death more frequently than whites accused of committing the exact same crimes. The report also indicates that nearly 80 percent of federal death row inmates are minorities. In fact, the report found that minorities account for "74 percent of the cases in which federal prosecutors seek the death penalty." The DOJ also concluded that the death penalty is applied in a "geographically arbitrary way," with certain states, like Virginia and Texas, accounting for most of the death penalty cases.

Despite these statistics, Dean has never acknowledged that the death penalty is racist in its application. For as Dean boasted in 1997 on through the summer of 2003: "Until life without parole means life without parole, the public is not safe without a death penalty. Until we have a judicial system that can adequately protect us, the only thing that will is the death penalty."

A State Approach to Gun Violence: It Won't Work

When one considers Dean's ignorance of the US death penalty, it seems that Sharpton's assertion that candidate Dean was "anti-black" may not have been far off the mark. But what about Sharpton's other claim—that Dean had a "pro-gun agenda?"

Dean believed that gun control issues should be handled at

the state level, not by the Federal government. "If I thought gun control would save lives in Vermont, I would [have] support[ed] it. If you say 'gun control' in Vermont or Tennessee, people think you want to take away their hunting rifle. If you say 'gun control' in New York or L.A., people are happy to see Uzis or illegal handguns taken off the streets," Dean said during his tenure as governor. "I think Vermont ought to be able to have a different set of laws than California. Let's keep and enforce the Federal gun laws we have, close the gun show loophole using Insta-check, and then let the states decide for themselves what, if any, gun control laws they want. We need to get guns off the national radar screen if Democrats are ever going to win again in the South and the West. Just as we resist attempts by President Bush to dictate … how we run our school systems and what kind of welfare programs to have, we need to resist attempts to tell states how to deal with guns beyond existing Federal law."

Unfortunately, Dean did not realize the lucrative status of the illegal interstate gun commerce. Out-of-state purchases account for the vast majority of assault weapons found in metropolitan areas such as New York City, Chicago, and Los Angeles. But Dean, who was endorsed by the National Rifle Association (NRA) eight separate times as governor of Vermont, contested, "The cross-border issue has been resolved in one case: Virginia now limits the availability of gun purchases because so many Virginia guns were turning up in New York City illegally." Dean was completely wrong, say anti-gun advocates, who insist that this issue has hardly been addressed.

"Governor Dean is wrong for America on gun policy," said Michael Barnes, president of the Brady Campaign to Prevent Gun Violence. "It makes no more sense to leave gun policy up to each individual state than it would to let each state set separate environmental standards. Guns cross state lines as easily as pollution. We're going to make sure that Americans who support our cause know he's wrong on these issues. Electing Howard Dean President would not be a step forward towards making our children and our communities safer from gun violence," Barnes emphasized during Dean's campaign. "We intend to make sure Americans know that."

Because gun traffickers attack dealers in the states with the weakest gun laws in order to obtain assault weapons, a state-by-state approach to ending gun crime will simply not work. And since gun traffickers typically sell these guns on the black market in metropolitan areas and in states with stricter gun laws, a Federal assault rifle gun ban is the only answer to help get illegal guns off the streets. As the Brady Campaign argues, "The only way to crack down on illegal gun sales is with strong Federal gun laws that apply to all states."

As Mary Leigh Blek, President Emeritus of the Million Mom March, put it: "We don't need a pro-NRA president. We've already got one. Americans who care about getting guns off our streets need to know there is virtually no difference between Governor Dean and President Bush."

Howard's Gay Folly

Many still claim Dean was a social liberal in Vermont; his signing of civil unions legislation in 2000 was a landmark event, after all. But as the debate over gay marriage has taught us, civil unions are not the same thing as "gay marriage." Dean, in fact, does not endorse any type of gay marriage; he, like Bush, believes such bonds are reserved for man and wife.

The Advocate, a gay culture magazine, quoted Dean during his bid for president as saying, "What the [civil unions] bill says is that marriage is between a man and a woman, but that same-sex couples have all the legal rights of marriage if they enter into a civil union … Civil unions have the legal impact we need to achieve equal rights under the law. I don't think same-sex marriage is necessary ... There are people in the gay community who think that's second-class citizenship. I don't agree, because in fact there is every right in a civil union there is in a marriage. It is true that it's a separate institution, but it is still equal."

As he did with regard to gun rights, Dean would relinquish this issue to state jurisdiction. "I think [gay marriage is] up to the people of each state," Dean said in an interview with *The Chronicle* in early December 2003. "We did not do gay marriage in Vermont. When I had the chance, we chose not to do it. But I'm not going to make a value judgment about the rights of other states to do what they want."

What Dean does not seem to understand is that, if left to the states, such legislation would never be fully implemented, as we have seen firsthand this past election year. Had the civil rights legislation of the 1960s been left up to the states, we would still have whites-only restaurants and government-endorsed race discrimination would still be widespread throughout much of the US.

All of the important technicalities aside, Dean did develop maverick civil union legislation in Vermont, didn't he? Well, not exactly.

In an April 2001 op-ed piece, Dean wrote:

> The Vermont Supreme Court in December of 1999 held that gay and lesbian people were not being provided with equal rights in our state. An hour and a half after that court issued its decision, I told the press and the people of Vermont that I would support a bill making our state the first in the country to provide all Americans with equality under the law.

But as *The Rutland Herald* editorialized in April 2000, shortly after Dean signed the legislation: "After the Supreme Court decision Dean's unease was evident. He acknowledged that the issue made him 'uncomfortable,' and his language, cautious and clumsy at the same time, reflected the unease many Vermonters felt in talking about homosexuality and gay rights."

In fact, the historic civil unions signing in Vermont only came to be after the Vermont Supreme Court pushed the issue and Vermont voters supported the measure. In the end, Dean was all but forced to sign the civil unions bill, which he did behind closed doors. If anything, Dean was simply doing his job, for which he should be commended, but the real credit for turning the tide goes to the Vermont Supreme Court and the Vermont voters who pressured the governor to sign the legislation into law.

Privacy Piracy

A year before Dean announced his bid for the presidency, he spoke at a Pittsburg event sponsored by a "smart-card" firm, Wave Systems. At the conference Dean announced that he hoped to one day implement a national identification card that would discourage online terrorism and identity theft.

"We must move to smarter license cards that carry secure digital information that can be universally read at vital checkpoints," Dean explained during his speech in March 2002. "Issuing such a card would have little effect on the privacy of Americans." Dean's Star Trek-like fantasy went as far as to state that the Federal government should mandate the implementation of ID card readers in all personal computers. The computer could then only be accessed once the system user inserted his or her national ID number into the security login.

"One state's smart-card driver's license must be identifiable by another state's card reader," said Dean. "It must also be easily commercialized by the private sector and included in all PCs over time—making the Internet safer and more secure."

"On the Internet, this card will confirm all the information required to gain access to a state (government) network—while also barring anyone who isn't legal age from entering an adult chat room, making the Internet safer for our children, or prevent[ing] adults from entering a children's chat room and preying on our kids ... Many new computer systems are being created with card reader technology. Older computers can add this feature for very little money," Dean said.

"In an age where identity and trust are paramount, the fact remains that the only viable form of universal identity in the US today is the state-issued driver's license," Dean added. "Think about it: When you entered the airport or the train station to travel to this conference, how many times did you use your driver's license to prove your identity? Remember—this is the same driver's license that teenagers alter in order to get into a club or buy cigarettes. Terrorists do it all the time. They did it on September 11."

Despite Dean's good intentions, such a card, if implemented, would pry into the private acts of individuals on their home computers. The government would be allowed to track all actions made by citizens via the Internet. Sounds like an Orwellian nightmare—one John Ashcroft would most certainly be ridiculed by privacy groups for endorsing.

"I'm from Vermont, and believe me, government is kept at a respectful but very conscious distance," Dean said. "Reality demands that we understand, first, that the rise of empowered individuals whose single mission is to destroy Americans means that we have to fight them at an INDIVIDUAL level and second—that we have already ceded our private information to faceless credit card companies and direct marketers who then sell it for a profit. Now—I believe that our nation has the technological capacity to protect both our privacy and our way of life."

He touted, "We will not, and should not, tolerate a call to erode privacy even further—far from it. Americans can only be assured that their personal identity and information are safe and protected when they are able to gain more control over this information and its use."

Although Dean may still contend that his ID vision is revolutionary, other civil liberty and privacy activists are skeptical such a system would actually protect privacy. Declan McCullagh quoted Barry Steinhardt, director of the technology and liberties program at the American Civil Liberties Union, as saying, "[Dean's idea] won't even work to protect against terrorism because we know that some of the 9-11 terrorists had phony driver's licenses that they were able to buy on the black market."

In the same January 26, 2004 News.com article, McCullagh quoted Chris Hoofnagle, the associate director of the Electronic Privacy Information Center: "I know of no other Democratic candidate who has this view on national ID. I hope that [Dean will] reconsider his policy on national ID because it has significant effects on individuals' right to privacy and does not make the country more secure. If you think about it, the implication is that children would have to be issued cards as well. Are we talking about ID cards from birth?"

The only response offered up by the Dean camp on this matter was, "No comment."

Dean on Dope

On August 15, 2000, Dean adopted the drug policy of the National Governors' Association (NGA), which states:

> To reduce the presence of illegal drugs, drug-related organized crime, and the adverse effects of drug and alcohol abuse in society requires a comprehensive strategy involving federal, state, and local governments. The Governors believe that one of the most severe public health threats is the recent rise in substance abuse among children.

The Federal Role

The profits from illicit drug trafficking can be effectively used to help state efforts to dry up the demand for these drugs. The nation's Governors urge the President and Congress to fully fund drug and alcohol abuse education, drug courts, treatment, prevention, and law enforcement efforts, including the initiative to combat and clean up methamphetamine production laboratories, at the state and local levels of government.

Intensified Eradication and Interdiction

Federal funding for use of the National Guard in drug and border enforcement deserves continued support. The Governors urge the President and Congress to utilize the role of US military forces in interdiction efforts.

High-Intensity Drug Trafficking Area Program

The HIDTA program provides additional federal funds to those areas to help federal, state, and local law enforcement organizations invest in infrastructure and joint initiatives to dismantle drug trafficking organizations. Governors support the HIDTA initiative and urge Congress to continue supporting the program.

The Federal Role in Reducing International Drug Trafficking

The nation's Governors urge the Administration and Congress to significantly tighten procedures for certifying foreign countries for eligibility to receive US aid based on their cooperation with US surveillance, interdiction, and eradication efforts.

Drug Legalization

> The nation's Governors believe illicit drug legalization
> is not a viable alternative, either as a philosophy or as a
> practical reality.

Dean's endorsement of the NGA's drug policy proves that he would not have altered the United States' approach to drug production and use. In fact, by endorsing the NGA's drug policy, Dean gave his stamp of approval for continuing the war on drugs and eradication efforts in Colombia and elsewhere. But as *CounterPunch* co-editor Jeffrey St. Clair puts it, "[Such] programs are a foolhardy way of addressing problems associated with drug consumption. It doesn't work, it oppresses the weak, and merely plays into the pockets of the drug profiteers, from the cocaine generals to the drug cartels and the banks who launder the money."

While Dean talks tough about drug proliferation as a health problem, his explicit misgivings regarding the use of medicinal marijuana were still apparent. In fact, Granite Staters for Medical Marijuana, a pro-medical-marijuana organization, gave Dean a "D-" rating—a score that was just marginally higher than the score they gave President Bush. To support its case, the group cited H. 645—Vermont's 2002 legislation, which would have allocated protection to seriously ill Vermont citizens from arrest and jail "for using medical marijuana with their doctors' recommendations."

During the time *The Rutland Herald* characterized Dean as "a staunch opponent" of the legislation, arguing that "H. 645 passed the Republican-controlled Vermont House by 82-59, and there were sufficient votes in the Democratic-controlled Senate to pass it there. But Dean used his influence with Senate leaders—who acknowledged that they didn't want to pass a bill that Dean would veto—to make sure it never received a floor vote. The legislature did eventually pass, and Dean signed a bill creating a task force to study the issue. The task force reported in early 2003 that medical marijuana patients deserve legal protection, but Dean's actions guaranteed that medical marijuana patients would continue to face arrest, leaving it to a future governor to fix this injustice."

So why did Dean thwart a medical marijuana bill during his tenure as governor?

"Let me tell you what we have to do on medical marijuana," Dean explained during a November 13, 2003 Town Hall meeting in New Hampshire. "Because I'm a doctor, I think substances taken into your body have to be treated the same if they're meant to be medicines, no matter what they are … I'm not in favor of legalizing marijuana—I mean, *maybe* (emphasis added) for medicinal use ... And so I'm not in favor of the kinds of raids that John Ashcroft is doing in those states where people have decided that medical marijuana is okay. I don't agree with the way it came about from a political process, but I'm not in favor of locking people up for medical marijuana like John Ashcroft is doing."

The Granite Staters for Medical Marijuana put it best: "[Dean] ignores the fact that the DEA does not raid individual cancer patients, as Dean seemed to claim. The current DEA policy is to raid hospice-like organizations that provide medical marijuana to patients. Dean left open the possibility that he would continue these cruel raids on caregivers that interrupt the flow of medicine to thousands of sick and dying patients."

The Reformer

During the 1990s, Dean levied restrictions for Vermont Medicare recipients under the guise of fiscal responsibility. According to *The San Francisco Chronicle* and the Associated Press, Dean claimed in 1993 that: "Medicare is the best argument I know why the federal government should never be allowed to run a national health care system." He was later quoted as saying,

"I think [Medicare is] one of the worst federal programs ever."

His statements puts him squarely to the right not just of progressives on this issue, but of the majority of Americans who favor a national health care system similar to Canada's.

During the heated primary race Dean's opponents pointed out that as governor, he supported Gingrich's plans to make senior citizens pay more and strip Medicare funding by up to $270 billion. As Dean said at the time: "I can tell you that the bureaucracy [is] associated with capitated care … far less than it is, for example, associated with Medicare, which is, from my point of view, a bureaucratic nightmare."

Dean also said, "I agree with [South Carolina Republican Gov.] Carroll Campbell when he says the federal government ought not to be allowed to administer a national health care program. They've already [proven] that they can't do that in a national health care program for those over 65, which is Medicare."

And according to a May 1992 *Rutland Herald* article, "As he has in the past, Dean stressed that the states must move ahead of the federal government in reforming health care. Medicare, which turns its recipients into 'second class citizens' and has been a fiasco for health care providers, is 'the best advertisement' for why the federal government must not be allowed to draw up the blueprint for national health insurance."

When it came time to balance his budget or eliminate the deficit, Dean often regarded social programs as secondary concerns. Of course, when Dean was criticized for his Medicare quotes from the 1990s during the primary debates, he retreated, insisting, "I spent 13 years of my life with senior citizens, and I can promise you that as president of the United States [I will ensure] not only [that] Medicare [will] not be cut but every senior citizen will have adequate health care. Medicare will be shored up, and every senior citizen will have a prescription benefit. I spent 13 years of my life doing this and I am not going to let us backslide now."

Not surprisingly, this move was a hallmark act in Dean theatrics, as the presidential candidate consistently shifted his policy stance on a number of issues, including international trade, pre-emptive war, gay rights, and the death penalty, among others.

He was also an adamant supporter of welfare reform. Jim Farrel wrote in a May 2003 issue of *The Nation*, Dean has "said some welfare recipients 'don't have any self-esteem. If they did, they'd be working' and scaled back Vermont's welfare program, reducing cash benefits and imposing strict time limits on single mothers receiving welfare assistance."

Dean recognized the dangers of creating new jobs under Vermont's welfare program. As he explained, "What we do that's different is we don't cut off all benefits; we cut off cash benefits, which means people don't get kicked out in the street." And in a 2001 Associated Press article, Dean surmised, "The biggest danger in this is people won't be able to find a job. If you can't find a job in our system you can continue to get your grant if you work in a public nonprofit or a private nonprofit job." Nonetheless, his support for Clinton's Federal program and Vermont's welfare program never waned.

Author and syndicated columnist Norman Solomon criticized Dean's welfare reform record in late 2003, writing, "While some other Democrats angrily opposed Clinton's welfare reform, it won avid support from Dean. 'Liberals like Marian Wright Edelman are wrong,' [Dean] insisted. 'The bill is strong on work, time limits assistance, and provides adequate protection for children.' Dean co-signed a letter to Clinton calling the measure 'a real step forward.'"

Though we now know that welfare reform was really a step backwards, hindsight is always 20/20. But even hindsight couldn't offer perfect vision for Dean, who never saw through the lies. On National Public Radio (NPR) in July 2003, he commended the Clinton administration's outlandish welfare policy, arguing that "What Bill Clinton did was appropriate … let's not forget that Bill Clinton ran on bringing health insurance to every single American and balancing the budget, really somewhat similar to the platform that I run on, and he won." But as a political nubile, Dean should have been reminded that, thanks to the President's fiscal stringency, Clinton's platform failed most poor Americans. Would Dean's platform have failed them as well? Indeed.

"I think welfare reform has been an incredibly positive force," Dean raved in an interview with the online journal *Liberal Oasis*. "Vermont was the first state in the nation to institute welfare reform, and we've had great success with it."

Chapter Eight

The Fall

Beltway Democrats Sink Dean For America

Doesn't all of this make you wonder what all the hype was about? As you now know, Howard Dean was a candidate from the Democratic mainstream. But despite his ideological alignment with the New Democrats, he did take them on, hoping to disrupt their stranglehold on Democratic politics. Dean was empowered. Not because he had a passion for progressive ideals, but because his followers led him down an alternative path. They saw Dean as a chance to challenge the Democrats for their conservatism. For that, Dean must be thankful, for the Deaniacs made him a substantial threat.

Immortalized as the reason for the plummeting of Dean's campaign is his famous scream after losing the primary in Iowa. The role the incident played reveals a great deal about how our media works, a topic to which we will return. Putting that aside for a moment, it is instructive to see how the Democratic Party dealt with him apart from the issue. The moves of the DLC reveal a great deal about how tight the control over the party is and how narrow the range of acceptable debate can be. The minimization of this so-called debate also reveals how the Democrats and their liberal cohorts enabled George W. Bush to win his reelection effort.

Howard Dean's campaign first took on water after Al Gore endorsed Dean for president on December 9, 2003. Hailed by many in the mainstream press as a huge boost to Dean's bid, the endorsement came at the same exact moment Democratic insiders were meeting to discuss how to sink his advances. For they knew he was a potential threat to the Clinton Democrats.

Theories of why Gore endorsed Dean spread like fire through

the media. As political commentator Adam Nagourney told Gwen Ifill on PBS's *Newshour* on the day of the endorsement: "One [theory] is that what is going on here is a proxy war between the Clintons and the Gores over the future of the Democratic Party. I think there is an element of truth to that. I don't think we want to exaggerate that."

He was right. The war had begun. Verbal bombs dropped— with one target in sight: the future of the Democratic Party. Dean was out for establishment blood, and Gore gladly went along for the ride. "Howard Dean was assassinated in broad daylight. Unlike Kennedy's 'grassy knoll,' Dean's killers are not hiding—it was the Democratic Party itself, and more specifically the Democratic Leadership Council, that successfully went after and sabotaged his candidacy ... The DLC reacted with fury to [Dean] ... going all out to torpedo his momentum," Naeem Mohaiemen correctly opined on Alternet.org following Dean's presidential death.

> Although Democratic nominees soon piled on the 'bash Dean' bandwagon, earlier attacks were carried out by DLC operatives. There was even the smell of scandal when two top Democratic candidates were found sharing information about Dean in an attempt to slow him down.
>
> But the great myth of the current [Howard Dean] cycle," DLC leaders Al From and Bruce Reed wrote in a May 15, 2003 memo, "is the misguided notion that the hopes and dreams of activists represent the heart and soul of the Democratic Party ... What activists like Dean call the Democratic wing of the Democratic Party is an aberration: the McGovern-Mondale wing, defined principally by weakness abroad and elitist, interest-group liberalism at home.

No doubt it was scandalous. But there was more to the drama than Dick Gephardt and John Kerry passing notes under the table and the DLC crying foul. In fact, Democratic insiders with deep ties to the DLC began funding campaign ads against Dean, hoping to bring his campaign to a screeching halt.

David Jones, an avid fundraiser and organizer for the Democratic National Committee and a staunch DLC patron who garnered money for centrist New Democrats like Bill Clinton and Al Gore, founded an anti-Dean group that ran vile ads attacking him early on in the Iowa contest. Deceptively called "Americans for Jobs, Health Care & Progressive Values, 2004 Election Cycle," Jones' group conducted a poll, which found that most Americans championed Dean's Iraq war stance. But few knew of his support of NAFTA, Medicare cuts in the mid 1990s, or his endorsements from the NRA.

"The first spot, on Dean's NRA endorsements, ran Dec. 5-12 in Iowa," *The Chicago Sun Tribune* reported on February 19, 2004. "The second ad ran Dec. 12-19 in Iowa and hit Dean on his NRA backing and NAFTA and Medicare stands. By this time, Jones did not have much money left."

Jones' group raised in excess of $600,000 from numerous Democratic insiders, including former New Jersey Democratic Senator Robert Torricelli, whose political career ended abruptly when he fell victim to ethics violations. Torricelli donated $50,000 to Jones' group.

As *The Washington Post* reported on February 16, 2004, "The [Jones' donor] list makes clearer than ever that the rules need to be changed to provide timely disclosure—to ensure that voters know who is behind this kind of attack advertising in time to factor that into their decision-making, should they so choose. We learn now that unions that had endorsed Rep. Richard A. Gephardt (Mo.) contributed $200,000 of the group's $663,000 in donations. Two top Gephardt backers also contributed: Leo Hindery Jr. of YES Network ($100,000), who served as a national finance co-chair, and Swanee Hunt ($25,000), who was a national campaign co-chair.

"While Mr. Gephardt's backers [including Jones during the

late 1990s] constituted the bulk of the donors, they weren't alone: Slim-Fast Foods founder S. Daniel Abraham, a major Democratic donor who contributed to his home state senator, Bob Graham (Fla.), and to Sen. John F. Kerry (Mass.), gave $100,000. J. McDonald Williams, a former chairman of the Trammell Crow construction company and a donor to the Bush-Cheney campaign this year, though to Democrats in previous cycles, gave $50,000 … Mr. Torricelli, you will remember, had the cash to spare because he was forced to quit his reelection race after being 'severely admonished' by the Senate Ethics Committee for accepting expensive gifts from a campaign donor he was doing official favors for. Now a champion at collecting special-interest money is gathering checks for Mr. Kerry, who's busy railing against those interests."

As it turns out, the *Post* article doesn't even tell the full story. In reality, the ties between Jones' organization, the Kerry campaign, and ex-DNC chair Terry McAuliffe were much stronger than suggested.

As Marc Brazeau pointed out on the online political site Joe Hill Dispatch, a closer examination reveals "that the law firm Skadden, Arps, Slate, Meagher & From was paid $18,000 for legal work by the group and the e-mail contact for Americans for Jobs" ended in skadden.com.

Why the fuss? It just so happens that skadden.com was the website for Skadden, Arps, Slate, Meagher & From, a firm that had donated $176,575 to John Kerry's presidential campaign as of mid-June 2004. To put things in perspective, this is more money than any other big Kerry backers, including Goldman Sachs, Citigroup, JP Morgan, and Microsoft, donated to Kerry's campaign as of October 1, 2004.

"And while the *Post* points out that Leo Hindery had ties to Gephardt, it should be noted that he testified before Kerry's communications committee as well.

"So you have a $50,000 contribution from Kerry fundraiser Robert Torricelli, legal expertise provided by Kerry's largest contributor, and a major donor from an industry that Kerry was responsible for regulating," Brazeau explained. "Those are the dots. Connect them how you like."

Given this, it's abundantly clear that the grassroots efforts of Howard Dean, Inc., were being taken on by insider money. Recognizing the challenge, Al Gore boarded the ship he hoped would not succumb to the rocky waters of Washington politics. But this scandal was just the tip of the iceberg, inevitably dashing Dean's prospects of winning his party's nomination as Democratic scorn prevailed.

DNC fundraising guru Terry McAuliffe was also ostensibly involved—perhaps directly—in Jones' anti-Dean propaganda. Leo Hindery, the former CEO of Global Crossing, donated $1,140,000 to the Democratic Party during the 2002 congressional race. Slim-Fast diet mogul S. Daniel Abraham, meanwhile, forked over $1,450,000 to the Democratic Party that same year.

McAuliffe tapped into these fat cats' resources, scoring a bundle of cash—some $18 million—for himself when he ditched his Global Crossing stock in 1999. But McAuliffe's tie to the anti-Deaniacs didn't end there. Along with McAuliffe, Bernard Schwartz, who donated $15,000 to Jones' group, was a plaintiff in a 1998 lawsuit over the alleged breaching of export regulations between the US and China.

In fact, Schwartz, the chairman and CEO of Loral Space & Communications, has a long history of complicity in Democratic scandals. In 1994, he gave the DNC $100,000 and visited China with President Clinton's Commerce Secretary Ron Brown. Their trip yielded an annual $250 million package for cellular telephone service in the country. Two years later in 1996, Schwartz wrote Clinton urging him to allow Loral to use Chinese rockets to launch their multi-million dollar satellite. The Chinese and Loral officials had been in negotiations since 1994, under the auspices of a contract Loral had with their contractor Intelsat. Schwartz was upset, as his Republican-backing competitors, Lockheed Martin and Hughes Aircraft, had been operating in China for some time.

Despite overt objections by the Defense Department and Secretary of State Warren Christopher, Clinton personally transferred jurisdiction of satellite-export licensing from the State Department to Commerce Secretary and ex-chairman of the DNC Ron Brown. At the same time, Schwartz increased his contributions to the Democratic Party, making him the largest single contributor in the 1996 election cycle. Later that same year Clinton signed a waiver that allowed Schwartz's Loral Space Company to export a satellite they had manufactured to China.

"[Schwartz] was honored on his 71st birthday with a private White House dinner. It's because of this access, Clinton's critics suggest, that the president rubber-stamped Loral's launches in China—even after Loral apparently ignored security procedures in 1996 by faxing Beijing a draft report about a Chinese rocket crash that destroyed a Loral satellite," Ken Silverstein wrote in *Mother Jones* in November 1998. "But campaign cash and personal ties are only the obvious way that Loral—and the defense industry—buys favors in Washington. An in-depth look shows that thousands of former Pentagon workers routinely go to work for arms makers and defense industry consultants upon their retirement, and confidential memos obtained by *Mother Jones* from such a company show how easily these cozy relationships influence legislation," Silverstein contended.

And in 2002, Loral paid $14 million to the State Department after Schwartz was charged with aiding the Chinese's missile technology research by faxing the draft report. Their payment was a sort of legal plea bargain intended to close the book on the 1996 matter. In July 2003, shortly after this payment, Loral went bankrupt. But thanks to a nudge from Republicans and their main advisory, Lockheed Martin, the company is now making its way back to the top. And while thousands of employees have since been laid off in Loral's Silicon Valley home because of the ordeal, Schwartz is—not surprisingly—still riding high.

Given that this is how big money works for "Washington Democrats," it is little wonder that Schwartz wanted to punish Dean for challenging the DC norm, even if the presidential hopeful had only stumbled into the role of "maverick progressive" by accident. The truth is, Schwartz didn't want this new base of Democratic activists to take over the party he did business with.

Evidently, Dean's movement scared the money-hungry Democrats right out of their thousand-dollar suits. McAuliffe, Reed, Kerry, Gephardt, and the Clintons were terrified of what he could do to the party they worked so hard to build during the 1990s. It didn't matter that Dean was ideologically aligned with these centrist Democrats—his grassroots cash was a genuine threat to party brass.

As DLC leaders Reed and From commented in another memo on Kerry's and John Edwards' successful campaigns in Iowa, "Two months ago, when former Gov. Howard Dean's campaign appeared to be running away with the Iowa caucuses, Sens. John Kerry and John Edwards spoke to the Iowa Jefferson-Jackson Day Dinner and made the same prophetic point: Democrats need to offer answers, not just anger."

"Now the Democratic wing of the Democratic Party has spoken: Iowa was a landslide victory for hope over [Howard Dean] anger. The word 'stunning' hardly does service to the performance of Kerry and Edwards in Iowa. Up against all of Howard Dean's endorsements and organization, Kerry and Edwards each won more delegate shares (the arcane measurement used to judge success in Iowa) than Dean and Rep. Dick Gephardt combined. Kerry's victory and Edwards' strong second weren't just stirring comebacks for those two campaigns. They represent an inspiring comeback for the Democratic Party.

"Iowa was also a triumph for a Democrat who wasn't on the ballot: the original Comeback Kid, Bill Clinton," they boasted. "The Dean campaign has done everything it can to run away from Clintonism, even calling the historic progress under Clinton nothing more than 'damage control.' By contrast, Kerry and Edwards followed the Clinton playbook ... While Dean defined himself as everything Bush is not, Kerry and Edwards set their own course for the country. They supported the war against Saddam Hussein and ... they also pledged muscular internationalism to unite the world against terror, a return to fiscal discipline and Clintonomics, bold plans to expand opportunity for the forgotten middle class.

"Indeed, the Iowa results represent a vindication for the Blair Democrats who supported the war in Iraq. Even Democrats with serious doubts about Iraq want America to succeed there, and want a nominee who can pass the test as Commander-in-Chief."

Al Gore and later Bill Bradley grasped their chances of taking on the Clinton-controlled DLC to which they once belonged, hoping to turn power over to the new iconic liberalism represented by the pro-Dean movement. To reassert the centrality of the party line, David Jones was brought on, albeit at a comfortable distance from the Kerry and Gephardt camps, to crush Dean's rebellious candidacy.

"Americans for Jobs, Healthcare and Progressive Values ran at least three ads in December against then-Democratic presidential front-runner Dean in early-voting states," the Associated Press reported on February 10, 2004.

"The group spent $15,000 on an ad aired in South Carolina and New Hampshire that showed a picture of bin Laden and said Dean lacked the experience needed to take on terrorists."

Some in the Dean campaign saw what was happening. The AP quoted his spokesman, Jay Carson, as characterizing Jones' anti-Dean commercials as "some of the nastiest smear ads" in the history of the Democratic Party.

"The Washington establishment put this group together just to try to stop Gov. Dean," claimed Carson. Jones pompously bragged, "We did more with $600,000 than Howard Dean did with $41 million."

Jones, no doubt, was right.

Media Killed the Political Star

Instead of organizing on the street and going door-to-door in Iowa like they should have done, Dean's campaign manager Joe Trippi and team attempted to play ball with the big boys. The weapon of choice for Trippi and his opposition was none other than the mass media. Trippi couldn't handle the TV ads. But David Jones could. Unfortunately, as Team Dean quickly discovered, focusing the majority of the campaign's energy on Internet activity had clear limitations. Given that the Internet had not previously been used to raise cash and garner political support, Dean's popularity was difficult to gauge. In fact, because the Internet was such an innovative source for mobilizing enthusiasts, Dean's message did not reach many traditional voters in Iowa. Trippi, noticing the gap late in the game, decided to speak to these folks through their television sets. But they weren't tuning in.

Once Trippi derailed Dean's ability to propagate his campaign platform, defeat was a near-certainty. Jones' PR machine was already in high gear, putting together their anti-Dean barrage. But the first negative ad that aired in Iowa was an advertisement developed by Trippi's firm, which depicted Dean berating Gephardt for his stance on the Iraq war.

October 2002. Dick Gephardt agrees to coauthor the Iraq war resolution, giving George Bush the authority to go to war," the background voice in the TV ad murmured. "A week later, with Gephardt's support, it passes Congress. Then last month, Dick Gephardt votes to spend $87 billion more on Iraq. Howard Dean has a different view." Howard Dean then chimes in, "I opposed the war in Iraq, and I'm against spending another $87 billion there. I'm Howard Dean, and I approve this message because our party and our country need new leadership.

Gephardt countered Dean with his own flagrant advertising assault. "Howard Dean is attacking Dick Gephardt for a position Dean took himself," the announcer says before the ad cuts to a question asked of Dean during the September 15, 2003 primary debate:

> "Is that an up or down, yes or no, on the $87 billion per se?"

> Dean: "On the $87 billion for Iraq?"

> Questioner: "Yes."

> Dean: "We have no choice, but it has to be financed by getting rid of all the President's tax cuts."

> Gephardt then pops on the screen, announcing, "I'm Dick Gephardt, and I approve this message because leadership is about making tough decisions and sticking with them."

The rest of the Iowa pack, particularly Kerry and Edwards, avoided the brutal attacks against one another, focusing their energy instead on the Bush administration and allowing the Jones crew and Gephardt to make Dean the target of Democratic attacks. This degree of infighting so early in the race was unprecedented in the Democratic Party. And since these ads aired in Iowa, no Democrat cast other candidates in a negative light in any TV spot. Why would they? Dean and Gephardt came in a distant third and forth, as the smooth-talking DLC-backed Kerry-Edwards duo moved to number one and two respectively, proving the effectiveness of negative advertising.

Around the same time a libertarian group called Club for Growth ran a TV ad where two actors pretending to be an older Iowa couple said that Dean "should take his tax-hiking, government-expanding, latte-drinking, sushi-eating, Volvo-driving, *New York Times*-reading...body-piercing, Hollywood-loving, left-wing freak show back to Vermont. Where it belongs."

Following his more-than-embarrassing third place finish in Iowa, Dean, hoping to rally his base, gave his now infamous screaming speech that became the media pinnacle for his downfall.

Eric Salzman, reporting for CBS News on January 26, 2004, wrote:

> The media is having a great time with Howard Dean's 'concession' speech in Iowa … Like a horrific car accident on the side of the road, the clip of Dean listing the states with early primaries, and ending with a gleeful 'yalp,' is hard not to watch, even if there is nothing to gain from seeing it … What you might not know, because it doesn't play 30 times a day on the cable news channels, is what was happening in the rest of the room. You don't see the visual, and you don't hear the audio. The television crews recording the event plug into an audio source picking up Dean's microphone, not the sound of the room. The cameras focus in to a tight shot of the candidate, not the rest of the room. What you are not hearing is a room with thousands of people screaming and cheering. What you are not seeing are hundreds upon hundreds of American flags waving.
>
> What you are not hearing are members of the audience shouting out state names urging Dean to list more. What you are not seeing is the way Dean's supporters were lifted out of their slump by the speech.

But never mind what really happened. The media was

having a hay-day with Dean's tantrum. The unelectability of the governor, cast as a maniacal demon, was played out every half-hour on the cable news networks. And fellow Democrats loved the negative takes on the scream. "You've heard of mad cow disease? This was mad candidate disease," *The San Francisco Chronicle* quoted Garry South, a senior adviser to Senator Joe Lieberman, as saying. "I sat there in total disbelief. It was beyond anything I'd ever seen," South said. "If I were Trippi and (Dean pollster Paul) Maslin, I would have been having a heart attack." It was truly the first thick nail in Dean's campaign coffin.

Although the DLC was astonished at Dean's ranting yelp, they were nonetheless pleased. Everything Jones and his ilk wanted was coming true. Dean was self-destructing. And he was nudged to that brink by his own party's elite establishment.

New Hampshire came next. Dean was already on the downward slide after Iowa, but his gang had hoped they could climb back into the saddle and ride off with a victory in the New England state.

Everybody in the Dean campaign knew New Hampshire was critical for Dean. Most didn't know that Trippi was planning on leaving the campaign regardless of whether Dean won or lost. He had nothing more to offer. If Dean didn't come in second or a close third, he would be finished for good. But many in the Dean camp still felt confident. The Governor remained steady in the polls, although his numbers declined substantially after the Iowa ordeal. His troops had been in the state for months, attempting to organize and get out the Dean message. Certainly his frightening speech didn't help. And by now Dean's wife Judith had been dragged before the TV cameras, on display for the media doctors to dissect. This spectacle was clearly in poor taste, and her uncomfortable demeanor did not bode well for Dean, who was working hard to get past his Iowa outrage and show the country he was just a normal fella, who just happened to hate GW Bush. So he pulled on a wool sweater and stomped to work in snowy New Hampshire.

None of these maneuvers mattered, however. Dean lost by double digits, an embarrassing finish indeed.

Marcus Teesey, a Dean volunteer in New Hampshire wrote of his experiences and his views on Dean's collapse in the state:

> The Dean machine was a brigade-sized organization that rapidly and suddenly—and in my opinion unexpectedly—acquired the enthusiastic support of ten divisions' worth of new people through Meetup. Not all, but a definite majority, of these people had no political experience ... People whose campaign experience was limited to stuffing envelopes and holding signs got important staff jobs in New Hampshire. The enthusiasm was there and so was the intelligence, but the core competence wasn't and isn't universal ... If Dean had had a year to build his New Hampshire campaign with the resources available at the time of the primary, things would have been much smoother. Communications errors wouldn't have occurred. Chains of command would have been clearer. Many thousands of man-hours were wasted in New Hampshire due to these things, which went some way towards nullifying the numerical advantage Dean's organization held over Kerry's. The rest of the way was because Kerry's field grunts were, as a group, far more experienced than Dean's.

There's an important lesson in Teesey's tale: Winning the presidency, like any large political victory, takes a great deal of time and planning, a long-term project that Dean compressed into a fatally short-term campaign. A progressive—or even a liberal like Dean—who wants to be president should be laying the groundwork for 10 or more years in order to get it right.

Dean went on to lose all of the primaries before dropping out after his defeat in Wisconsin. Trippi resigned after New Hampshire, inspiring Dean to bring on Washington insider and Bill Clinton's close friend Roy Neel as his replacement. It was a sign of what was to come for Dean the Democrat who would fall back into the party line, leaving his followers to traverse the Kerry trail instead. He did pick up delegates by winning his home state of Vermont well after he quit, but by then it was far too late to matter.

Dean hadn't made it to half of the states he had screamed out while on the mic following Iowa. To put it mildly, many Deaniacs were disenfranchised, as they struggled to understand what had gone awry.

Was it poor organizing? The media? Trippi? Dean's persona? They needed to point fingers at those they blamed for his demise.

Some correctly accused Beltway Democrats, who from the inception of Dean's campaign wanted to derail his hopes. The DC scoundrels were not expecting such massive anti-war support for the lackluster Vermonter. Surely DNC chief McAuliffe was never in touch with the resentment that was brewing on the ground leading up to Bush's war on the Iraqi people. Trying to funnel that anger back to Washington was no easy task for these anti-warriors, but many saw Dean as the only way to effectively challenge the party that had overwhelmingly gone along with Bush's preposterous attack and subsequent occupation. These perceptive activists gathered through the virtual world and planned their own assault on Bush. Surely they had the energy, but they were not prepared for the harassment their candidate would receive from party bigwigs.

This is what leads us to the larger story: the difficulties of taking on the corporate entrenched Democrats who believe the best way to win elections is to continue moving rightward. Although Dean was a centrist and conservative in almost every regard, he still operated on the political margins while running for president. He didn't raise his funds in the normal corporate circles. He challenged the system and was supported by Americans far more progressive than he was.

Many of Dean's patrons believed him to be progressive, a sort of Ralph Nader of the Democratic Party. But Dean, as you have read, was no Nader, or even Dennis Kucinich for that matter. He was, and continues to be, a New Democrat ideologically. Perhaps Dean was correct when he said he didn't know what to expect. He had no idea Washington Democrats would not welcome him with open arms. He thought he was one of them. However, they hated him, and despised his followers even more.

In fact, that is why it is so appalling that Dean began campaigning for Kerry after his defeat. Roy Neel had been successful. He, like other conventional Democrats, didn't want Dean's activists to stray from the party, even though the Democrats would never embrace their beliefs. They have and always will take progressives and even most liberal-minded voters for granted. That's been the part the Democrats—long the graveyard of radical social change—have played for the past 40 years.

On Friday, June 9, 2004, Dean stepped into the ring with independent presidential candidate Ralph Nader. The old consumer advocate hardly flinched as Dean repeated half a dozen times that we must do everything in our power (that is, legal power) to rid the country of the Bush plague. We are in a state of "emergency," he boldly announced.

Obviously reincarnated after his own presidential death, Dean went so far as to claim that John Kerry had "progressive credentials." That is clearly something you would have never heard quiver off the lips of Dean the candidate, who himself lacked credentials of the progressive stripe. But Dean was now the defender of the party that did its best to slaughter him during the primaries. He had become the poster boy for a lousy Democratic ticket, which set him up for the future within the party establishment.

Looking back on Dean's record, it was no surprise that he defended Kerry's candidacy. "Many Democrats also admire Ralph Nader's achievements as I do," Dean said shortly after Nader announced his candidacy. "But if they truly want George Bush out of the White House, they won't vote for Ralph Nader in November." Unfortunately, Dean forgot to mention that Kerry and the Democrats never planned on bringing real transformation even if Kerry had won, which we'll get to later.

The Dean saga shows just how far right we are politically in the US. Many have theories as to how this gross Democratic mindset unfolded, but the fact is, this trend is here to stay, and working within the party—though noble in some regards— cannot produce genuine shifts in ideological values, especially at the national level. Regrettably, even when there are signs that progressive challenges will alter the *status quo* of Washington politics, they all die a not-so-pleasant death.

Part II

With Friends Like These…

The General

Another Measure of American Desperation

with Sunil K. Sharma

W hen liberals and some progressives offered their enthusiastic support for front-running Democratic presidential contenders Wesley Clark and Howard Dean during the peak of the primary season, it became evident that oppositional politics were in a dismal state in these United States of America. Support for the candidates ranged the full spectrum of the establishment left, from publications like *The Nation*, to former Vice President Al Gore, to liberal celebrities like Michael Moore.

With decades of unremitting right-wing assaults on every sphere of American life having succeeded in jerking the political and cultural landscape to the right, the main battlecry coming from "the left" in the 2004 election season was the "Nobody but Kerry," better known as the "Anybody But Bush" (ABB), spectacle.

But the "Anybody" in that statement meant "anybody with a realistic chance of winning the election." Long before the first primary, the genuinely progressive platforms of Democratic candidates such as Al Sharpton and Dennis Kucinich had been deemed unrealistic and unworthy of consideration not only by the media but also by liberal activists and advocacy groups who often conceded privately that they preferred a Dennis Kucinich, Al Sharpton, or Ralph Nader.

Amidst almost daily reports of American soldiers killed in a brutal war, many Americans are realizing that they have been deceived into supporting Bush's bloody foray. Certainly the war was made under false pretenses. A catastrophic error. At the same time the US launched its offensive, the rich in America were receiving lavish tax breaks as services benefiting the common good were eviscerated. It is little wonder that Bush's popularity ratings were constantly in a flux. In this degraded political climate, simply declaring oneself an anti-war, anti-Bush candidate promised to draw cheers from a battered opposition. And while the Democratic options might have been a minor improvement over Bush, our standards have proven to be so degraded that most progressives get weak in the knees as business-as-usual candidates like Clark and Dean somersault over such a low hurdle.

Another White Knight from Little Rock

Four-star general Wesley Clark first commanded public attention as the Supreme Allied Commander of NATO during the US war on Serbia in 1999, and as a CNN military analyst up until September 2003. Early in 2004, a grassroots campaign to draft Clark to run for the presidency formed and, thanks to the wonders of the Internet, garnered many signatures. When Clark received a letter from left-liberal author and filmmaker Michael Moore urging him to run for president after the famed liberal met the general at a private New York shindig, Clark's campaign got a significant—albeit unanticipated—boost. According to Moore, his letter helped generate 30,000 letters to the "Draft Clark" campaign and, sure enough, a few days later Clark declared his candidacy.

Because he was a general whose anti-Bush positions on Persian Gulf Slaughter II, the Patriot Act, and other reactionary policies could not seriously be deemed "unpatriotic," "anti-American," or "crazy," Clark was for a short while considered "our best hope" to defeat Bush in 2004. But a closer look at the past of the real Wesley Clark makes us wonder why so many liberals and erstwhile progressives like Moore went gaga over Wes. And more importantly, this grotesque display tells us something about the superficial nature of politics on the left, where many were so willing to embrace such a candidate.

Clark's decision to run as a Democrat was an odd development, and his allegiance to the party was questionable at best. Not only did Clark cast his first presidential vote for Richard Nixon, but he also voted twice for Ronald Reagan and George Bush the Elder. Up until 2002, Clark was delivering speeches at GOP fundraisers in his home state of Arkansas, fuelling speculation he was considering a run for the Oval Office as a Republican. In a speech he delivered at a fundraiser for the Pulaski County Republican party on May 11, 2001, Clark praised Ronald Reagan's Cold War policies which created a huge military build-up, Bush Sr.'s foreign policy that slaughtered Iraqis in the first Gulf War and singled out the current administration's hyper-unilateralist national security team, boasting: "We're going to be active, we're going to be forward-engaged. But if you look around the world, there's a lot of work to be done. And I'm very glad we've got the great team in office: men like Colin Powell, Don Rumsfeld, Dick Cheney, Condoleezza Rice, Paul O'Neill—people I know very well—our president, George W. Bush. We need them there because we've got some tough challenges ahead in Europe."

It is embarrassing to see progressives falling for such politics—and for someone who essentially waffled on his political allegiances.

Clark only declared himself a Democrat in August 2003. Why the decision to run as a Democrat? A hint can be found in a September 29, 2003 edition of *Newsweek*. After 9/11, Clark had expected the Bush administration to enlist him in its "War on Terror." As the article explained:

> [Clark had] been NATO commander, and the investment firm he now worked for had strong Bush ties. But when GOP friends inquired, they were told: forget it. Word was that Karl Rove, the president's political mastermind, had blocked the idea. Clark was furious. [Clark] happened to chat with two

prominent Republicans, Colorado Gov. Bill Owens and Marc Holtzman ..."I would have been a Republican," Clark told them, "if Karl Rove had returned my phone calls." Soon thereafter, in fact, Clark quit his day job and began seriously planning to enter the presidential race—as a Democrat. Clark late last week insisted the remark was a "humorous tweak." The two others said it was anything but. "He went into detail about his grievances," Holtzman said. "Clark wasn't joking. We were really shocked."

"Anti-War" Ain't What it Used to Be

So why were liberals and progressives so enamored with Clark? Part of Clark's appeal stemmed from the widespread perception that, as Michael Moore wrote in his aforementioned letter, Clark "oppose[s] war." But as the media watchdog group Fairness and Accuracy In Reporting (FAIR) revealed in a review of statements made by Clark before, during, and after the Iraq war, if Clark was "anti-war," the term had clearly been gutted of any meaning:

*   In an article published in *The Times* of London, April 10, 2003, Clark savored America's great "victory" over Iraq: "Liberation is at hand. Liberation—the powerful balm that justifies painful sacrifice, erases lingering doubt and reinforces bold actions. Already the scent of victory is in the air. Yet a bit more work and some careful reckoning need to be done before we take our triumph ... President Bush and Tony Blair should be proud of their resolve in the face of so much doubt."

*   As the US and its client Israel were beginning to focus their crosshairs on other Arab nations like Syria and Iran, we had Clark writing in the same article: "But the operation in Iraq

will also serve as a launching pad for further diplomatic overtures, pressures and even military actions against others in the region who have supported terrorism and garnered weapons of mass destruction. Don't look for stability as a Western goal. Governments in Syria and Iran will be put on notice—indeed, may have been already—that they are 'next' if they fail to comply with Washington's concerns."

Sounds like something straight out of the Project for a New American Century playbook.

Many Clark supporters were stunned when he told *The New York Times* on September 19, 2003, that he would have voted for the congressional resolution authorizing Bush to attack Iraq: "At the time, I probably would have voted for it, but I think that's too simple a question." After pausing to reconsider his statement, Clark repeated: "I don't know if I would have or not. I've said it both ways because when you get into this, what happens is you have to put yourself in a position—on balance, I probably would have voted for it."

In response to his supporters' shocked reaction to the "anti-war" candidate's statement, Clark quickly backpedaled, clarifying: "Let's make one thing real clear, I would never have voted for this war ... I've gotten a very consistent record on this. There was no imminent threat. This was not a case of pre-emptive war. I would have voted for the right kind of leverage to get a diplomatic solution, an international solution to the challenge of Saddam Hussein."

But Clark's oft-repeated claim that the US should act in concert with the international community to a reach a diplomatic solution on Iraq was belied by statements he made on CNN prior to the invasion:

*   "I probably wouldn't have made the moves that got us to this

point. But just assuming that we're here at this point, then I think that the President is going to have to move ahead, despite the fact that the allies have reservations." (1/21/03)

* "The credibility of the United States is on the line, and Saddam Hussein has these weapons and so, you know, we're going to go ahead and do this and the rest of the world's got to get with us … The UN has got to come in and belly up to the bar on this. But the president of the United States has put his credibility on the line, too. And so this is the time that these nations around the world, and the United Nations, are going to have to look at this evidence and decide who they line up with." (2/5/03)

And let's not forget that as Supreme Commander of NATO, Clark led an undeclared war against Serbia that was never approved by the UN. Before the Kosovo War commenced in March 1999, Clark repeatedly called for US air strikes against Serbia. Clark's claims that he had a consistent record were simply false.

Maximum Violence

It is instructive to look at Clark's actions during the Kosovo War as Supreme Allied Commander of NATO. "We're going to systematically and progressively attack, disrupt, degrade, devastate, and ultimately, unless President Milosevic complies with the demands of the international community, we're going to destroy his forces and their facilities and support," Clark insisted. As William Blum suggests, Clark bombed Serbia with "an almost sadistic fanaticism," making profligate use of deadly cluster bombs and depleted uranium, of the sort still ravaging Iraq. *The Washington Post* reported Clark "would rise out of his seat and slap the table. 'I've got to get the maximum violence out of this campaign—now!'"

Clark, of course, wasted no time in doing so. As he led a brutal air war against Serbia, Clark, who considered schools, bridges, hospitals, electrical facilities, market places, trains, refugee convoys, and media outlets "legitimate targets," delivered death and destruction primarily to civilians and their infrastructure, leaving the Serbian military relatively unscathed.

Independent estimates of the civilian death toll in the Kosovo War range from over 500-2,000, yet according to Clark's testimony before Congress, there were between 20 and 30 instances of what he called "collateral damage."

Clark's attempts to cover up instances of intentional NATO bombings of civilian targets had been exposed, though not properly publicized. In one case, 14 people were killed in Grdenicka, Serbia, on April 12, 1999, when a US jet bombed a passenger train crossing a bridge. Clark claimed the atrocity was a tragic mistake, as the pilot was firing on the bridge and the train only came into view after the bombs had been dropped. He showed two video films shot from the nose of the remote control-guided bombs to support his claim, which were later found to have been doctored. In fact, the train could be seen on the bridge when the pilot bombed it, and he turned around to make a second sweep on the burning bridge, dropping a bomb directly on the carriage.

***

The Wesley Clark story is just one more heart-wrenching exhibit of how the left deals with such "hopefuls" within the Democratic Party. Certainly many progressives in 2004 failed to deal with who these candidates really were. Even those who knew the genuine Clark, like respected columnist Norman Solomon (who donated $1,500 to the Clark campaign), still opted to make a strategic choice: "Vote for the Democratic nominee, whoever he or she is, because said candidate is at least marginally better than

George W. Bush."

Or so they claimed.

This was a difficult choice made by many on the left, including well-known and respected intellectuals and activists—including Noam Chomsky, Howard Zinn, Medea Benjamin, and Tim Robbins, among others—in order to expedite the process of removing Bush from power. However, we must be clear what the costs of expedient choices are, even if the benefits seem predominant. Backing the lesser evil, as the ABB crowd did in 2004, keeps the entire political pendulum swinging right.

Refuting the followers of the ABB faith, Independent presidential candidate Ralph Nader told Amy Goodman of *Democracy Now!* in early October 2004:

> It is a total loss of nerve. I mean, first of all, they didn't ask anything of Kerry. They said to the voters in the close states like Michigan, Wisconsin, Oregon ... vote for Kerry, quote, "even though we strongly disagree with Kerry on the war and other issues," end quote. Well, when you don't demand anything of Kerry, he gets worse. If you don't make Kerry better, he gets worse because the corporations are demanding 24 hours a day. They're not squeamish like the left is.
>
> More important is that if the left believes that their issues are compelling issues to the majority of the American people, they should be proud to pull Kerry toward them so he can get more votes. It's as if they're ashamed of their issues, like, gee, "living wage, that's a very important issue, but it's not a big vote-getter." Like full health insurance for all, that's very important. We want to pull Kerry in that direction. It's not like getting out of Iraq, where now a majority of people are saying it was a mistake to send the troops in, and 42% of the people want the troops back yesterday.
>
> Oh no, no, no. Don't pull him into this issue; "it's not a vote-getter." This is the collapse of the left ... They have

in effect put a figurative ring in their nose. They have said
to the Democrats, "Because the Republicans are so bad, we
collapse. We're going for the least-worse."

When you don't make any demands, when you engage
in unconditional surrender, why should Kerry ever look back
at you? Why should he give you the time of day?

John Kerry never ended up looking back at the members of
the left, let alone the rest of the liberal establishment that supported
him unconditionally. Instead, Kerry steamed forward (or rather,
backward) and lost a monumental election. He never differentiated
himself from Bush on the major issues and consequently the Kerry
campaign ended up aiding the Republicans, not the Democrats.

The Democrats couldn't galvanize swing voters, let alone
new ones, who could have easily altered the outcome of an election
where Bush should have been on the ropes and knocked to the mat
in the first round for his handling of the economy and the Iraq War,
among other transgressions.

Sadly though, the majority of the left caved and bought into
the ABB philosophy. Many, even those that knew what they were
voting for, still held their collective nose and voted for John Kerry
simply because he was not George W. Bush.

However, adherents to left principles would have been more
effective in changing the result of the 2004 election had they
pressured Kerry and the Democrats to take on the issues they
cared passionately about—which surely could have brought out
the vote to counter the impressive organizing achieved by the Karl
Rove and the religious right.

But what were these ABBers supporting anyway? We know
what they were voting *against*, but what were they voting *for*?

What follows are detailed illustrations of how the Democrats
laid the political groundwork for the policies that Bush has
advanced, as well as how the Democrats and their liberal patrons
failed to distinguish themselves from the Republicans and the

conservatives on a host of issues. Wesley Clark and Howard Dean are just two sketches in a much larger portrait of Democratic disappointments.

These overt failures have indeed helped elect many Republicans, including George W. Bush in 2004.

Chapter Nine

Mourn, But Don't Mythologize

Thoughts on the Death of Paul Wellstone

with Sunil K. Sharma

S o why can't we just focus on building up the liberals within the Democratic Party? Why not simply support *real* "progressives" like the late Senator Paul Wellstone of Minnesota or those who will no doubt take his place in a long line of politicians working within the party to help take it over? Without diminishing respect for the dead, Wellstone's career reveals a great deal about the limits of even the so called "progressive wing" of the Democratic Party.

Since Paul Wellstone's tragic death over two years ago in an October 25, 2002 plane crash, tearful remembrances have poured forth in articles and commentaries across the nation, especially in left-liberal media publications.

Widely regarded as an outspoken progressive in the Senate, Wellstone was a tireless voice for the "little fellers, not the Rockefellers" of America. His death "silenced one of the strongest voices for minority members and progressives" in the corridors of power, giving them "pause about who will champion their interests in the inner circles of party leadership."

Many also perceived Wellstone to be the spokesperson for the movement to stop a second Iraqi war. Wellstone's influence on the movement was evident at the massive anti-war protests across the US on October 26, the day after the Senator's death.

In San Francisco and Portland, Oregon, where both of us attended rallies, banners, placards, and speakers lamented the fallen anti-war hero. Some quarters of the left were fraught with prolific speculations that foul play was behind Wellstone's death.

While the following may sound insensitive—even malicious—that certainly is not our intent.

Immediately after the death of presidents Richard Nixon and more recently Ronald Reagan, the mainstream press bent over backwards to overlook their many sins, allowing Tricky Dick and the Gipper to be canonized overnight. Rather than emanating exclusively from the right, the whitewash was also the product of mainstream liberals and lefty pundits across the country.

The left, of course, is not immune from this sort of custom either. John F. Kennedy, for instance, launched the invasion of South Vietnam in 1961-1962, approved chemical warfare against the South Vietnamese, initiated the murderous Alliance for Progress in Latin America, backed military coups throughout the so-called Third World (or initiated what successors later finished), and signed off on fiscally regressive policies that favored the super-wealthy. Yet many leftists continue to romanticize Kennedy as a shining knight stolen from us by the dark forces of intoxicated reaction.

Similarly, Wellstone was not the eminent "progressive" many liberals and leftists made him out to be. He may have been liberal in the context of the American ruling elite, but given the extreme rightward drift in the US over the last 30 years (where many lament Nixon as the last domestically liberal president), that's not saying a whole hell of a lot.

Though Wellstone could have stood behind Senator Russ Feingold—one of the few Democrats to cross party lines and vote in favor of Attorney General John Ashcroft—in opposing the USA Patriot Act, he didn't.

Wellstone also supported the US war against the Taliban in Afghanistan.

His opposition to the then looming war on Iraq was qualified and essentially unprincipled. He believed the US should not have acted unilaterally, implying that the invasion would have been justified if the UN had supported American aggression.

"We should act forcefully, resolutely, sensibly—with our allies, and not alone—to disarm Saddam," Wellstone said in *The Jewish Telegraph* in October 2002. "Authorizing the pre-emptive, go-it-alone use of force now, right in the midst of continuing efforts to enlist the world community to back a tough new disarmament resolution on Iraq, could be a costly mistake for our country."

A strong supporter of Sharon's Zionist Israel, Wellstone had also "signed or co-sponsored various congressional letters in support of Israel." As the *Minneapolis Star Tribune* reported on October 20, 2002, "The American Israel Public Affairs Committee (AIPAC), the leading pro-Israel lobbying group, has told its members that Wellstone voted the pro-Israel position on 20 of the last 21 votes they rated. The lone exception was a 51-49 vote that broke down along party lines."

Wellstone continually betrayed his early 1990s pledge to fight for a single-payer health care plan after being cowed by Hillary Clinton.

Despite these pitfalls, Wellstone voiced significant opposition to Clinton/Bush's Plan Colombia, the $1.3 billion US aid package to the Colombian death-squad government. Wellstone's political stance on other issues was also relatively stable, but in the aggregate Wellstone could hardly be described as a "progressive" unless the term now merely means "liberal pragmatist."

Equivocating the definition of progressive as such inflates or misrepresents a person's legacy, thereby deflating progressive causes. Because effective popular action requires a sober analysis of reality (in this case, Wellstone's own veracity), lionizing or mythologizing a politico is potentially disempowering. That is, such a practice lends itself to the mistaken notion that positive change can come from "good" leaders, rather than what historically has been the source of positive change: progressive grassroots movements, working together, creating and snowballing populous action in times of conflict.

One writer's comments on IndyMedia following Wellstone's death summed it up best:

> If you want to mourn Wellstone, do so because another human being died a needless death—NOT because he was some kind of champion of progressive politics, which is increasingly becoming a non-existent entity within the US political establishment itself. The only champion of progressive politics you will find is within yourself—or not at all.
>
> Moreover, if you want to mourn Wellstone because you believe that he died under shady circumstances which deserve to be fully investigated, then do so. Indeed, this aspect of the story is one which deserves to be examined more fully as it obviously has great political ramifications in terms of political control of the US federal government— rather than a whitewashed eulogy of Wellstone's political career and politics.

And so as we organize and struggle in these dark days to fight for peace and social justice, let's do it with our eyes open and without illusions—and perhaps, without the Democrats.

Chapter Ten

Richard Holbrooke and East Timor

Bipartisanship in American Diplomacy
with Merlin Chowkwanyun

Those who cast a presidential vote for John Kerry in hopes of altering the US foreign policy paradigm may have wasted their energy. What the mainstream media and others failed to disclose this past election season was that one of Senator Kerry's key foreign policy advisors, Richard Holbrooke, happened to play a significant role in perhaps the largest US-backed genocide of the last century.

Kerry brought Holbrooke on board, as *The Washington Post* put it on October 22, 2004, to "repair global alliances and attract new allies to assist in Iraq." The *Post* also reported that if Holbrooke was not awarded the hotly sought after position of Secretary of State, Kerry would have at least "sent [him] to the Middle East as a special envoy as a possible consolation prize."

Holbrooke's role in the Kerry campaign exemplifies the fact that the Democrats are continuing to move rightward. The progressive community should have been condemning Kerry about the potential appointment of Richard Holbrooke. But instead liberals gave a premature endorsement, which helped fuel the rightward drift of the Democratic Party by assuring Kerry that his positions would have no effect on the support he received from the left end of the political spectrum.

In 1975, during Gerald Ford's administration, Indonesia invaded East Timor and slaughtered 200,000 indigenous Timorese. The Indonesian invasion of East Timor set the stage for a long and bloody occupation that was ended when an international peacekeeping force was introduced in 1999, following the Clinton administration's six years of military support for Indonesia. Clinton had waited patiently until Indonesia's army had burned East Timor to the ground before finally severing all military ties in the late nineties.

Recent transcripts of meetings among Indonesian dictator Mohamed Suharto, Gerald Ford, and his Secretary of State, Henry Kissinger, conclusively show that Kissinger and Ford authorized and encouraged Suharto's murderous actions. "We will understand and will not press you on the issue [of East Timor]," Ford said in a meeting with Suharto and Kissinger in early December 1975, just days before Suharto's bloodbath. "We understand the problem and the intentions you have."

At the meeting Kissinger also stressed that "The use of US-made arms could create problems," clarifying, "It depends on how we construe it; whether it is in self-defense or is a foreign operation." Kissinger continued, "It is important that whatever you do succeeds quickly." Kissinger's concern, clearly, was not about whether US arms would be used offensively but whether the act could be construed as illegal under international law.

After Gerald Ford's loss and Jimmy Carter's ascendance into the White House in 1976, Indonesia requested additional arms to continue its brutal occupation of East Timor, in spite of a ban on arms trades to Suharto's violent government. It was Carter's appointee to the Department of State's Bureau of East Asian and Pacific Affairs, Richard Holbrooke, who authorized additional arms shipments to Indonesia during this supposed blockade. According to many scholars, this was the period when the Indonesian suppression of the Timorese reached genocidal levels.

When he testified before Congress in February 1978, Professor Benedict Anderson cited a report that proved there was never a US arms ban. In fact, he explained, during the period of the alleged ban the US initiated new offers of military weaponry to the Indonesians:

> If we are curious as to why the Indonesians never felt the force of the US government's 'anguish,' the answer is quite simple. In flat contradiction to express statements by General Fish, Mr. Oakley, and Assistant Secretary of State for East Asian and Pacific Affairs Richard Holbrooke, at least four separate offers of military equipment were made to the Indonesian government during the January-June 1976 'administrative suspension.' This equipment consisted mainly of supplies and parts for OV-10 Broncos, Vietnam War-era planes designed for counterinsurgency operations against adversaries without effective anti-aircraft weapons, and wholly useless for defending Indonesia from a foreign enemy. The policy of supplying the Indonesian regime with Broncos, as well as other counterinsurgency-related equipment, has continued without substantial change from the Ford through the present Carter administrations.

If we track Holbrooke's statements over the past few years, the disturbing symbiosis between him and figures like the hawkish Paul Wolfowitz, whom Kerry supporters enjoyed invoking when demonizing Bush, is startling.

"In an unguarded moment just before the 2000 election, Richard Holbrooke opened a foreign policy speech with a fawning tribute to his host, Paul Wolfowitz, who was then the dean of the Johns Hopkins School of Advanced International Studies in Washington," reported *First of the Month* following the 2001 terrorist attacks.

The article continued:

> Holbrooke, a senior adviser to Al Gore, was acutely aware that either he or Wolfowitz would be playing important roles in the next administration. Looking perhaps to assure the world of the continuity of US foreign policy, he told his audience that Wolfowitz's 'recent activities illustrate something that's very important about American

foreign policy in an election year, and that is the degree to which there are still common themes between the parties.' The example he chose to illustrate his point was East Timor, which was invaded and occupied in 1975 by Indonesia with US weapons—a security policy backed and partly shaped by Holbrooke and Wolfowitz. 'Paul and I,' he said, 'have been in frequent touch to make sure that we keep [East Timor] out of the presidential campaign, where it would do no good to American or Indonesian interests.'

In short, Holbrooke worked vigorously to keep his bloody campaign on the down low. The results appear to have paid off, as few Kerrycrats and ABBers expressed qualms about Holbrooke's role in Kerry's foreign policy platform, which will surely be resurrected if Kerry runs again in 2008. In his own chilling words, Holbrooke described the motivations behind his support of Indonesia's genocidal actions:

> The situation in East Timor is one of a number of very important concerns of the United States in Indonesia. Indonesia, with a population of 150 million people, is the fifth largest nation in the world, is a moderate member of the Non-Aligned Movement, is an important oil producer—which plays a moderate role within OPEC—and occupies a strategic position astride the sea lanes between the Pacific and Indian Oceans ... We highly value our cooperative relationship with Indonesia.

Chapter Eleven

The War Path of Unity

Democrats Ignore the Peace Movement

> "I will be voting to give the President of the United
> States the authority to use force—if necessary—to disarm
> Saddam Hussein because I believe that a deadly arsenal of
> weapons of mass destruction in his hands is a real and grave
> threat to our security."
>
> *Sen. John F. Kerry, D, MA, Oct. 9, 2002*

Although it was indeed sad, it was not surprising that
Dennis Kucinich, the feisty liberal Representative from
Ohio who ran—or hobbled—for the Democratic presidential
nomination would roll over and play dead for Senator John Kerry
just days before the 2004 Democratic Convention in Boston.
"Unity is essential to bring change in November," announced
Kucinich on July 22, 2004. "Unity is essential to repair America.
Unity is essential to set America on a new path."

Despite Kucinich's emphasis on the importance of "unity,"
it wasn't exactly clear what his "new path" mantra was all about.
After all, Kucinich delegates failed (though they never really had
a chance) to make "immediate troop withdrawal from Iraq" a
central plank in Kerry's narrow platform just one week earlier.
Kerry, of course, promised to put more troops in Iraq, call on
NATO to intervene in the occupation, and essentially be a more
kick-ass administrator of Bush's egregious foreign policy than the
neo-cons had been.

The second Democratic presidential candidate to abandon
his anti-war base, Kucinich allowed his candidacy to be absorbed
back into the dank establishment sponge. Just months earlier

Howard Dean embarrassingly touted the novel Democratic line of "unity at all costs," snarling in late March 2004, "In the end, it is Generation Dean voting for John Kerry for president of the United States that is going to send George Bush back to Texas, where he belongs."

Like Dean, Kucinich urged his former supporters not to succumb to Ralph Nader's tempting anti-war allure even though John Kerry did not oppose the war in Iraq or the ongoing occupation. "I intend [to] reach out on behalf of the Kerry-Edwards ticket to unite our party with all those who may have felt left out," he contended. "I will let them know that the time has come to unite in a common effort for change, which is essential, not only for America but for the world."

Meanwhile, many Kucinich delegates at the convention felt dejected. Initially, the man for whom they had devoted much time and energy intimated that he would "release" them, paving the way for their robotic votes for Kerry.

Later, after hearing impassioned (and tearful) testimonies from his delegates, Kucinich changed his mind, and told them to "vote their conscience." Fair enough. But most ended up voting for Kerry regardless. And what did they receive in return for their candidate and most of their delegates' support for Kerry? Not much.

Despite the generally symbolic role of the platform in modern politics (Bush in 2000 infamously bragged that he had never read the GOP platform), seventeen Kucinich platform demands were axed in exchange for a borderline illogical statement with no indication of an exit strategy or an impending pullout from Iraq. It pledged to remove troops "when appropriate so that the military support needed by a sovereign Iraqi government will no longer be seen as the direct continuation of an American military presence."

Absent from the platform was support for Palestinian rights, homosexual civil unions and marriage, as well as repudiation of the pre-emptive war doctrine in principle and as executed in Iraq.

"I ask you, are millions of anti-war/anti-occupation Americans welcome in the Democratic Party? If such voters are indeed welcome, I urge you to demonstrate this by permitting debate within the party on the war and occupation issue, both in Miami and in Boston," wrote Jessie Jackson, prior to campaigning for John Kerry, who said nary a word about the exponential proliferation of the racist prison-industrial complex, increasing poverty, or black male unemployment, now over 50% in New York City alone.

The Democratic National Convention itself was a difficult affair for many who attended. As polls indicated, 80-90% of the attending delegates declared themselves anti-war. Those trying to express such a view quickly received the muzzle.

Charles Underwood, the only Minnesota Kucinich delegate to vote for Kucinich, told Amy Goodman's radio program *Democracy Now!:* "I am just very disappointed that there is no ability to express any hope for peace on the floor of this convention. We have had our signs confiscated, we've had our scarves for peace, you know, 'Delegate For Peace,' confiscated. We have had people that tell us to sit down and be quiet."

Meanwhile, the anti-war delegates were not lucky enough to hear any speeches at the DNC that reflected their point of view and were instead presented with two gung-ho militaristic orations.

Vice presidential candidate John Edwards told the anti-war delegates: "We will always use our military might to keep the American people safe. And we, John and I, will have one clear unmistakable message for Al Qaeda and these terrorists. You cannot run. You cannot hide. And we will destroy you."

Move Over, MoveOn

MoveOn, the liberal online advocacy group that backed both Howard Dean and Dennis Kucinich, had also been asking its members, who overwhelming opposed the Iraq war, to donate cash and time to the pro-war Kerry campaign.

Following the release of Michael Moore's *Fahrenheit 9-11,* the organization sent an e-mail plea to its constituents. "This is the moment for us to send Kerry a powerful message, one he'll want to hear. The more we show Kerry that real people with strong, progressive values are key to his success, the more strongly he'll fight for our values as President ... it's an especially good time to reinforce that we value this kind of leadership from John Kerry. Help send this message now by giving to his campaign through the link below."

MoveOn was at least attempting to put pressure on John Kerry, you say? Unfortunately, an organization can't donate money to a campaign without articulating certain demands, and MoveOn's demands were far too meager.

When I emailed MoveOn staffer Noah Winer regarding the role he wanted his organization to play if Kerry prevailed in the election, he responded, "It's a big question, and I don't think anyone can answer it unless it becomes a reality. It will take time and member input to find that new role. MoveOn will certainly continue to work on the issues our members care about, no matter who is elected."

So I emailed Noah back and asked him whether MoveOn would be as hard on a Kerry administration as it has been on Bush, for Kerry would certainly continue the illegal Iraq occupation. Winer failed to reply.

Lacking any visible remorse just like Dean and Kucinich, MoveOn alienated its huge anti-war base, continuing to operate under the illusion that progressively garnered PAC funds could influence Kerry or any of the other New Democratic elite. Waging this futile effort, MoveOn should've known better.

History was not on their side. Prior to the Iraq war, for instance, MoveOn, hoping to stop Bush's imminent assault, organized meetings between its members and US senators. Few senators attended the gatherings, leaving their underlings and MoveOn spokespeople to debate this heated subject. Predictably, few listened, and most ignored the activists' distress.

Despite what the spin-doctors say, Democrats are largely to blame—not only for discounting the peace movement but also for laying the groundwork Republican hawks needed to justify attacking Saddam's regime and waging Bush's greater "War on Terror."

Bipartisan Aggression

As Democratic Leadership Council kingpins and proponents of Bush's war Al From and Bruce Reed wrote in the July 2004 issue of *Blueprint* magazine, "In the 1990s, Bill Clinton showed Americans once and for all that Democrats could make the economy grow again, make government work again, and make America safe again. As a tough-minded internationalist and decorated war hero, Kerry has a chance to make his own mark, and complete the transformation of the Democratic Party as the one Americans can trust to make the nation stronger both at home and abroad."

What From and Reed failed to acknowledge was that bin Laden, on Clinton's dutiful watch, allegedly masterminded the 1993 attack on the World Trade Center (WTC) in New York City as well as the attacks on the US Embassies in Kenya and Tanzania in 1998. The CIA claimed the strikes on these buildings were carried out by the same ring of thugs that hit the USS Cole in October 2000, killing seventeen, and masterminded the horrific terror attacks in September of 2001, which intelligence officials concur were being planned well before Al Gore's 2000 defeat.

In 1993, Clinton himself bombed Iraqi intelligence centers for what he said was in retaliation for the attempted assassination of George Bush, Sr. "He said publicly that the US strike on Iraqi intelligence headquarters was retaliation for Saddam's attempt to kill (ex-president) George Bush," Laurie Mylroie, who worked as Clinton's Iraq specialist during his 1992 campaign, told WABC Radio's Steve Malzberg. "[But] he also meant it for the Trade Center bombing."

"Clinton believed that the attack on Iraqi intelligence headquarters would deter Saddam from all future strikes against the United States," she claimed. "It was hopelessly naïve."

It was also off the mark, for it wasn't Saddam that allegedly struck U.S targets, but Osama.

Then in 1996, Clinton bombed Iraq yet again. *Eat the State!* explained the pretense:

> Kurdistan, home of ethnic Kurds, was divided by colonial powers early this century into land now belonging to Iran, Iraq, Turkey, Syria, and a handful of former Soviet republics. Power in the portion of Kurdistan within Iraq's borders is divided primarily among two factions, hostile to each other and both hostile to Saddam Hussein. One faction got lots of arms from Iran recently and started to attack and overrun the other. Fearing for their lives, the other side asked their enemy, Hussein, to intervene and restore the original balance. Responding to a request from Iraqi citizens, who were under attack from a foreign-supplied army, Hussein moved some of his troops into the area, re-secured it, and withdrew.

Orchestrated by the Clinton administration in early September 1996, the bombings walloped several civilian targets and military facilities—without the approval of the UN or any international alliance, for that matter. The Iraqi government reported dozens of deaths and millions of dollars worth of damages. Sound familiar?

Of course, this wasn't a first for Bill Clinton, who had already been sadistically cruel to the children of Iraq. As the United Nations Food and Agriculture Organization reported a year earlier in 1995, as many as 576,000 Iraqi youth died as a result of United Nations sanctions that the US had imposed and supported since 1991. This conservative tally did not include the over 90,000 annual hospital deaths that the World Health Organization estimated would have not happened had Clinton not compelled the UN to enforce harsh sanctions against the Iraqi people. Sadly, it seems the litmus test for US presidential aspirants must include the will to brutalize Iraqi citizens.

In 1998, Clinton retaliated for an East African US Embassy bombing by firing 70 cruise missiles at a suspected bin Laden terrorist training camp in Afghanistan and heaving 17 missiles at a pharmaceutical plant in the Sudan. But as author and activist Howard Zinn explained in *Z Magazine* following the episode: "[Clinton] claimed that the Sudanese target was a plant producing nerve gas, but could not produce convincing evidence for this … Almost immediately, it became clear that the plant, contrary to the American claim, had been producing half the medicines used in Uganda." Needless to say, countless people died.

Later that year when Clinton signed into law the Iraq Liberation Act—drafted by the same hawkish neo-cons, including Republican staffer Randy Scheunemann, Donald Rumsfeld, former-CIA director R. James Woosley, and Ahmad Chalabi, that helped thrust forth Bush's own Iraq policy into law later that year—the US outlined its ultimate objective for its involvement in Iraq. That is, extinguishing the life of Saddam Hussein and his government.

It was as if DC already had the champagne on ice; regime change was so close, Congress could almost taste the after-party.

The House of Representatives overwhelmingly supported the legislation, and the Senate voted unanimously in favor of the bill.

When Clinton signed the legislation in mid-October 1998, Republican Senator Trent Lott sang his praises: "The Clinton Administration regularly calls for bipartisanship in foreign policy. I support them when I can. Today, we see a clear example of a policy that has the broadest possible bipartisan support. I know the Administration understands the depth of our feeling on this issue. I think they are beginning to understand the strategic argument in favor of moving beyond containment to a policy of 'rollback.' Containment is not sustainable. Pressure to lift sanctions on Iraq is increasing—despite Iraq's seven years of refusal to comply with the terms of the Gulf War cease-fire. Our interests in the Middle East cannot be protected with Saddam Hussein in power. Our legislation provides a roadmap to achieve our objective."

In what many criticized as an effort to deflect attention from his impeachment trial, Clinton tried his luck with Saddam one more time two months later on December 16, 1998. But unlike previous Iraqi bloodbaths, which paled in comparison, this attack was waged with primitive anger. As President Clinton asserted in a national televised address on the day of the first US offensive, "Earlier today, I ordered America's armed forces to strike military and security targets in Iraq. They are joined by British forces. Their mission is to attack Iraq's nuclear, chemical and biological weapons programs and its military capacity to threaten its neighbors ... Their purpose is to protect the national interest of the United States, and indeed the interests of people throughout the Middle East and around the world."

"Six weeks ago," he continued, "Saddam Hussein announced that he would no longer cooperate with the United Nations weapons inspectors called UNSCOM. They are highly professional experts from dozens of countries. Their job is to oversee the elimination of Iraq's capability to retain, create, and use weapons of mass destruction, and to verify that Iraq does not attempt to rebuild that capability … The international community had little doubt then, and I have no doubt today, that left unchecked, Saddam Hussein will use these terrible weapons again."

But as M.I.T. linguistics professor Noam Chomsky responded, "I think the major reasons [for the use of force] are the usual ones. The US and its increasingly pathetic British lieutenant want the world to understand—and in particular want the people of the Middle East region to understand—that 'What We Say Goes,' as Bush [Sr.] defined his New World Order while the missiles were raining on Baghdad in February 1991. The message, clear and simple, is that we are violent and lawless states, and if you don't like it, get out of our way. It's a message of no small significance. Simply have a look at the projections of geologists concerning the expanding role of Middle East oil in global energy production in the coming decades … The manner and timing of the attack were also surely intended to be a gesture of supreme contempt for the United Nations, and a declaration of the irrelevance of international law or other obligations; that too has been understood. The bombing was initiated as the Security Council met in emergency session to deal with the crisis in Iraq, and even its permanent members were not notified."

Surely Iraq had been brutalized for decades under the thumb of Saddam Hussein. But Clinton only escalated the cruelty. Writing for *Guardian Unlimited* in 2000, journalist John Pilger lamented:

> Six other children died not far away on January 25 last year. An American missile hit Al Jumohria, a street in a poor residential area. Sixty-three people were injured, a number of them badly burned. 'Collateral damage,' said the Department of Defense in Washington. Britain and the United States are still bombing Iraq almost every day: It is the longest Anglo-American bombing campaign since the second world war, yet, with honorable exceptions, very little appears about it

in the British media. Conducted under the cover of 'no-fly zones,' which have no basis in international law, the aircraft, according to Tony Blair, are 'performing vital humanitarian tasks.' The ministry of defense in London has a line about 'taking robust action to protect pilots' from Iraqi attacks—yet an internal UN Security Sector report says that in one five-month period, 41 percent of the victims were civilians in civilian targets: villages, fishing jetties, farmland and vast, treeless valleys where sheep graze. A shepherd, his father, his four children and his sheep were killed by a British or American aircraft, which made two passes at them. I stood in the cemetery where the children are buried and their mother shouted, 'I want to speak to the pilot who did this.'

This is a war against the children of Iraq on two fronts: bombing, which in the last year cost the British taxpayer £60 million. And the most ruthless embargo in modern history. According to UNICEF, the United Nations Children's Fund, the death rate of children under five is more than 4,000 a month—that is 4,000 more than would have died before sanctions. That is half a million children dead in eight years.

The irony is that the US helped bring Saddam Hussein's Ba'ath party to power in Iraq, and that the US (and Britain) in the 1980s conspired to break their own laws in order, in the words of a Congressional inquiry, to 'secretly court Saddam Hussein with reckless abandon,' giving him almost everything he wanted, including the means of making biological weapons. Rubin failed to see the irony in the US supplying Saddam with seed stock for anthrax and botulism, that he could use in weapons, and claimed that the Maryland company responsible was prosecuted. It was not: The company was given Commerce Department approval.

Denial is easy, for Iraqis are a nation of unpeople in the West, their panoramic suffering of minimal media interest; and when they are news, care is always taken to minimize Western culpability. I can think of no other human rights issue about which the governments have been allowed to sustain such deception and tell so many bare-faced lies. Western governments have had a gift in the 'butcher of Baghdad,' who can be safely blamed for everything. Unlike the be-headers of Saudi Arabia, the torturers of Turkey and the prince of mass murderers, Suharto, only Saddam Hussein is so loathsome that his captive population can be punished for his crimes.

This disaster in fact laid the groundwork for George W. Bush's Iraq invasion. It also took John Kerry down a tough road during the 2004 campaign, as the Democrats had actually done Bush's job for him in Saddam country. How could Kerry oppose what had already been done by his own party regarding Iraq? The Democrats had been just as much to blame for the mess in Iraq as the Republicans.

Following the decision by Bush and the Democrat-controlled Senate to take out the Taliban in Afghanistan by attempting to nab suspected 9/11 mastermind Osama bin Laden, Howard Zinn again reflected: "We can all feel a terrible anger at whoever, in their insane idea that this would help their cause, killed thousands of innocent people. But what do we do with that anger? Do we react with panic, strike out violently and blindly just to show how tough we are? 'We shall make no distinction,' the President proclaimed, 'between terrorists and countries that harbor terrorists.' Will we now bomb Afghanistan, and inevitably kill innocent people, because it is in the nature of bombing to be indiscriminate, to 'make no distinction?' Will we then be committing terrorism in order to 'send a message' to terrorists? We have done that before. It is the old way of thinking, the old way of acting. It has never worked. Reagan bombed Libya, and Bush [Sr.] made war on Iraq, and Clinton bombed Afghanistan and also a pharmaceutical plant in the Sudan, to 'send a message' to terrorists. And then comes this horror in New York and Washington. Isn't it clear by now that sending a message to terrorists through violence doesn't work, [that it] only leads to more terrorism?"

In retrospect, it is evident that Clinton and his Democratic cohorts did more than their fair share of laying the groundwork for Bush's war against and occupation of Iraq and Afghanistan. Not only did Clinton construct the political leverage Bush needed by signing the 1998 Iraq Liberation Act, but he also provided a model for Bush's relentless bombing of Iraq as he led several significant strikes on Afghanistan and the Sudan.

So when Bush began talking about regime change in Iraq, those who looked to the Democrats to halt the offensive were seeking out the wrong allies.

Bush's Iraq Attack

On October 10, 2002, the House of Representatives voted 296-133 in favor of giving Bush the green light to punish Saddam. Standing shoulder-to-shoulder with President Bush on the White House lawn, Dick Gephardt, who helped draft the measure, explained, "I believe we have an obligation to protect the United States by preventing [Saddam] from getting these weapons and either using them himself or passing them or their components on to terrorists who share his destructive intent."

Meanwhile, Bush was amassing support for his war in the Senate. Helping Bush's cause was Tom Daschle, the Democrat Majority Leader at the time, who surmised that Saddam's threat "may not be imminent. But it is real. It is growing. And it cannot be ignored." Hitching a ride on the war-wagon New York Senator Hilary Clinton added, "In the four years since the inspectors left, intelligence reports show that Saddam Hussein has worked to rebuild his chemical and biological weapons stock ... his missile delivery capability, and his nuclear program. He has also given aid, comfort, and sanctuary to terrorists, including Al Qaeda members. It is clear, however, that if left unchecked, Saddam Hussein will continue to increase his capacity to wage biological and chemical warfare, and will keep trying to develop nuclear weapons."

Buying Bush's war propaganda hook-line-and-sinker, the Democrats were all too eager to support the Iraq war. They believed Saddam had weapons of mass destruction and joined with Republicans in using it as a pretext to support aggression. They were convinced he was a threat to US sovereignty. They even thought Saddam had ties to Osama bin Laden. The donkeys were bewildered.

As far back as 1998, President Clinton articulated his concerns about a possible Iraq threat, announcing after a Pentagon briefing, "If Saddam rejects peace and we have to use force, our purpose is clear. We want to seriously diminish the threat posed by Iraq's weapons of mass destruction program." It should come as no surprise that Senators John Kerry, Tom Daschle, and Carl Levin wrote President Clinton that same year to illuminate the threat Saddam allegedly represented, emphasizing, "We urge you, after consulting with Congress, and consistent with the US Constitution and laws, to take necessary actions, including, if appropriate, air and missile strikes on suspect Iraqi sites, to respond effectively to the threat posed by Iraq's refusal to end its weapons of mass destruction programs."

The tide it seemed had a window of opportunity to turn away from this prelude to war, but predictably, the Democrats on their heels and hoping not to lose control of the Senate in a congressional election year, cowered in 2002. Although Rep. Kucinich perceptively saw the looming war as a momentous error and organized opposition in the House—some 133 votes—his decent effort failed.

With political interests and propaganda in mind, most establishment Democrats ignored his rationale, leaving the millions of protestors who took to the streets across America prior to the invasion with few representatives in Washington, historically or otherwise. And as the story goes, Bush easily got his way, much to the protesters' chagrin: On March 19, 2003, US forces rattled Baghdad with a military conquest like no other seen in history. The warmongers proudly dubbed their lethal deed "Shock-and-Awe."

By then, the Democrats, who had failed to articulate any basis for citizens to vote for them as opposed to their Republican rivals regarding the Iraq situation, had lost control of the Senate as well as many seats in the House. They didn't challenge Bush on any major issue. They supported his invasion of both Afghanistan and Iraq. It was a horrific display of political ineptness. The Democrats—unlike the millions of Americans who knew Bush and Co. had ulterior motives for unilaterally attacking Iraq—had been eager to back an illegal war.

By mid-summer 2004, the US death toll in Iraq had reached well over 1,000, with soldiers dying at a pace that far outnumbered the Vietnam War at its comparable stage. Tens of thousands of innocent Iraqis had perished; millions more mourned the loss of loved ones. There were no WMDs hiding beneath Iraq's turbulent soil. Saddam didn't have ties to bin Laden's gang after all. Iraq had posed absolutely no threat to the United States, let alone its neighboring countries, which did not support the US invasion.

Bush and the Democrats' war had played right into the terrorists' hands. According to intelligence reports, and bin Laden himself, recruitment for such groups escalated almost exponentially. The ensuing level of hatred toward the US was unprecedented.

Needless to say, claims that this war has made the United States—and we the people—any safer are laughable. Democratic henchmen Al From and Bruce Reed must have been hallucinating when they proclaimed Kerry would protect America from all that is evil. Kerry, of course, has proven to be no different from Bush on foreign policy issues, save for the 'D' next to his name on the ballot in 2004.

An aggressive unilateral policy only breeds terrorism, and Kerry's foreign policy would have only nurtured future terrorist activity, as Bush's is surely doing now.

Unfortunately, the same cretins continue to control the Democratic platform. They dictate what is or is not acceptable discourse within the party. Being anti-war, as we know, is most definitely unacceptable, which explains why those who listened did not hear Kerry breath even the faintest sigh of peace rhetoric along the campaign trail.

Although 82% of registered Democrats believed the war to be a grave mistake, according to a 2004 USA Today/CNN/Gallup Poll conducted on June 21-23, Kerry was steadfast in his support for the Iraq war. His own campaign platform was a glaring memento of the Democrats' inability to offer significant alternatives to George W. Bush. They simply believed they could manage the situation more astutely. "This administration did not build a true international coalition," Kerry's campaign platform proclaimed. He simply would have done it better.

In the context of a party hell-bent on war, whose foreign policy is essentially identical to the Republican policy, it doesn't matter how many MoveOn members donate money to the Democratic Party. In the end such reformers are left with nothing. No party. No money. No hope. And—perhaps worst of all—no unity.

Chapter Twelve

Partisan Protests

Clinton's and Bush's War on the Poor

My partner Jessica and I finalized our move from Brooklyn to Albany, New York, in late August 2004. We were forced to move and follow the money, as they say. While we filled our U-Haul with various odds and ends, gritty white hipsters from South Williamsburg were convening to protest the neo-cons' arrival in the Big Apple for the dreadful Republican National Convention. I was upset that I couldn't join them. I wanted nothing more than to drop the boxes I was carrying and raise my fist in dissent against an administration that has an appetite for, well, destruction.

As I watched these protesters amass, however, I noticed something peculiar. Most of my fellow Williamsburgers convening on the street seemed unconcerned that George W. Bush was using their city to host the Republican National Convention. They didn't give a shit that Bush was about to exploit the tragedy of September 11 to promote his reelection campaign. They were not angered by the whole charade. Not in the least.

At first I was perplexed. "Why aren't these folks, poor black and Latino minorities, on the frontlines raging against Bush and his band of thugs? They certainly have ample reason," I thought. "In fact they have more reasons than these 20-somethings, myself included, who will forever have the gift of white skin as a saving social grace. Why the overt political apathy?"

But then it hit me: Perhaps they don't see a point in protesting only one sect of the ruling elite while ignoring the other. Their problems are systemic, and yes, bipartisan in origin. Bush is only a symbolic figurehead of a corrupt, corporatized state. They don't need C. Wright Mills to point it out. They witness it—and live it—daily.

Surely, they know it was Bill Clinton who signed welfare reform, or as the Democrats called it, the "Personal Responsibility and Work Opportunity Reconciliation Act," not Bush. In fact, it is hard to imagine Bush getting away with signing a piece of legislation into law as horrid as the bill passed under Clinton and Gore. In fact, under Bush, Democrats have halted the reauthorization of welfare reform on three different occasions. Where was this defense under Clinton? Don't think so many would have watched silently had it been Bush who signed it into law in 1996. It is the "end of welfare as we know it," Clinton declared. How right he was.

"[M]ajor research studies now report that welfare reform harms families. Young children are going hungry, rushing to emergency rooms, being hospitalized and being abandoned at higher rates," welfare expert Sanford F. Schram wrote in 2002. "A personal responsibility act that simply pushed single mothers into low-wage jobs without making any provision for the care of their children was a contradiction in terms—it was irresponsible. It was immoral. It still is, and now the evidence proves it."

"It is disturbing that substantial numbers of children and families are sinking more deeply into poverty when we have the strongest economy in decades and when substantial amounts of funds provided to states to assist these families are going unused," Wendell Primus of the non-partisan nonprofit Center on Budget and Policy Priorities stressed in 1999. And things have only gotten worse. Both at home and abroad.

After all, under Clinton, the World Trade Organization (WTO) enhanced its strength, piquing the anger of tens of thousands of protesters, myself included, who took to the streets of Seattle in 1999, to demonstrate against the WTO's global supremacy.

Clinton also bolstered the influence of the International Monetary Fund (IMF) in the developing world and passed the

North American Free Trade Agreement (NAFTA), receiving few qualms from liberals and many progressives. It's no coincidence that neo-liberalism is now dictating the free-market economy despite the claims of some who argue that neo-liberalism has declined under Bush.

For those who were caught up in a love affair with Kerry's Democrats, beware: It was under Bush—not Clinton—that the US briefly challenged the WTO's legitimacy over steel imports. Bush eventually lifted the tariffs, but he held out longer than expected. While it is conceivable that Kerry (or Al Gore) would have done the same, the Senator is no doubt an ardent free-trader, particularly compared to Bush, who, unlike the New Democrats, is somewhat hesitant to embrace such neo-liberal dogma.

Although Bush supports the expansion of NAFTA into CAFTA (Central American Free Trade Agreement) and the FTAA (Free Trade Areas of the Americas), his administration has not made these free trade pacts a top priority like Clinton and Al Gore did in the 1990s with NAFTA.

This reality stands in stark contrast to the fabulous label we hear whenever Democrats defend Clinton's economy, which we will get to momentarily.

My old New York neighbors must also know first-hand that it was under Bill Clinton that the gap between the rich and poor reached historic levels, making it harder for these people to dig their way out of entrenched poverty. It was Democratic presidential candidate John Kerry who wanted to put more cops on the streets to crack some minority heads—which would have inevitably sent more non-violent individuals from poor neighborhoods like South Williamsburg into the prison industrial system, which expanded almost exponentially during the Clinton years. In fact, it was Clinton's 1994 Crime Bill that put 300,000 new inmates in an already grotesquely overcrowded and hyper-violent prison system and sent 100,000 new cops out on the streets.

The bill also expanded the death penalty by 58 offenses, and Clinton boasted in *Between Hope and History*, "We expanded the application of the death penalty for nearly sixty violent crimes ... And we have stiffened sentences for drug offenders and told those involved with drug activities in public housing projects they only get one strike. Public housing is a privilege; abuse it and you're out."

These poor Americans have few, if any, allies in Washington. Their votes are typically ignored, if even counted, and presidential aspirants like John Kerry rarely speak to their needs—even if Kerry's ex-Veep John Edwards smiled his way through his "Two Americas" speech. These folks weren't biting.

Iraq was not a major issue either. But why would it be? No one can be surprised that America has launched yet another imperial war. Many of my former neighbors hail from Puerto Rico, where they know the wrath of American stewardship first hand. Heck they are still fighting for statehood. For them, Iraq is just another chapter in a long history of American aggression.

Regardless of who won the November election, their struggles would surely continue: Finding adequate work. Providing their hungry children food. Health care that doesn't put them in the poor house. A solid education that leads to opportunities for their kids. And the list goes on.

As Jessica and I passed with our oversized mattress in hand, I heard one elderly man sitting on an overturned bucket say to his friend, "I bet these protesters wouldn't be doing this if that Kerry were in town." He was right, of course. It was a keen observation of our political reality in 2004—the ABB syndrome.

The majority of protesters who assembled in NYC to rail the GOP would not have thought of taking to the streets of Boston to battle the Democrats for their acceptance of "everything Bush" just one month prior. Not only was it cool to be anti-W, which was the major ABB draw, it was also intellectually appealing. At least for the selective-minded spectator. Most New York City ABBer's believed it was their duty to protest the RNC. Bless 'em. I would have been there if I could have, and I am sure many marching through the streets of Midtown knew the Democrats were to blame for much of what has transpired. But after seeing another segment of America that had ample reason to hate Bush sit back and laugh at the hipster upheaval in Williamsburg that day, reality reflected a slightly different picture of the RNC and the first four years of Bush era.

The problems plaguing America, and Fallujah for that matter, are *not* the fault of the neo-cons alone. Bush has acted on policies laid out by Clinton and the New Democrats in the 1990s.

With their faces painted, the protesters who passed my girlfriend and I as we packed our belongings in the back of our rented truck may not understand this. But the guy on the bucket and the other Brooklynites who seemed indifferent to the Republican takeover of NYC continue to see through the perpetual lies. They know 100,000 protesters in the streets is a good thing. I bet they just wish such dissent was not partisan in nature. If it were not, I'm sure they'd be arm-in-arm with their gentrifying neighbors.

The Economics that Put Them There: It's the Democrats' Fault

So let's get back to the notion that things were better for these hardworking folks economically under Clinton than they were Bush. Also we'll look at whether or not Kerry really would have been better than Bush for these people had he pulled off a win. This certainly seems to be the current belief on the left. However, the economy under Clinton may not have been as robust and healthy as we would like to believe. And Kerry may have done little to reverse the Bush-Clinton-Bush downward trend.

As economist Robert Pollin of the University of Massachusetts at Amherst explains in *Contours of Descent: US Economic Fractures and the Landscape of Global Austerity*, Clintonomics was not all it was cracked up to be. "The distribution of wealth in the US became more skewed than it had at any time in the previous forty years," he argues. "No question, an increasing number of US jobs began to be outsourced at an unprecedented rate as well."

"Unlike Clinton, Bush is unabashed in his efforts to mobilize the power of government to serve the wealthy," he continues. "But we should be careful not to make too much of such differences in the public stances of these two figures, as against the outcomes that prevail during their terms of office … the ratio of wages for the average worker to the pay of the average CEO rising astronomically from 113-to-1 in 1991 under Bush-1 to 449-to-1 when Clinton left office in 2001."

Pollin points out that while Clinton's tax policy reversed some of the regressive taxation that occurred under Ronald Reagan, it certainly did not reverse the brunt of it. And, as Pollin contends, "The fact is that, insofar as the end of the Cold War yielded any peace dividend under Clinton, it took the form of an overall decrease in the size of the federal government rather than an increase in federal support for the programs supposedly cherished by Clinton, such as better education, improved training, or poverty alleviation."

Was Clintontime even a boom-era after all? Pollin doesn't think so. "Under the full eight years of Clinton's presidency, even with the bubble ratcheting up both business investment and consumption by the rich average real wages remained at a level 10 percent below that of the Nixon-Ford peak period, even though productivity in the economy was 50 percent higher under Clinton than under Nixon and Ford. The poverty rate through Clinton's term was only slightly better than the dismal performance attained during the Reagan-Bush years."

Bargaining power for low-wage workers during the 1990s

decreased tremendously as well. Wall Street scion Alan Greenspan in fact did not want the unemployment rate to drop below 6 percent because he feared that inflation would skyrocket. Greenspan also did not want workers to increase their bargaining power, which could possibly benefit their organizing strength in the workplace. The majority of workers during Clintontime were not happy with their occupations.

As Pollin writes, "Wage gains for average workers during the Clinton boom remained historically weak, especially in relationship to the ascent of productivity. These facts provide the basis for the poll findings reported in *Business Week* at the end of 1999 that substantial majorities of US citizens expressed acute dissatisfaction with various features of their economic situation."

Pollin also shows that the Earned Income Tax Credit (EITC), the most significant economic initiative under Clinton, more than doubled from $9.3 billion to $26.8 billion during Clinton's first two terms. But food stamps "dropped by $8.5 billion reflecting a large increase in the percentage of households who are not receiving food assistance even though their income level is low enough for them to qualify. Under the Clinton administration, the decline in the number of people receiving food stamps—9.8 million—was 17% greater than the decline in the number of people officially defined as impoverished and was accompanied by a dramatic increase in the pressure on private soup kitchens and food pantries.

"And while the EITC does correct some of the failings of the old welfare system, it has created new, and equally serious, problems. Moving poor and unskilled women from welfare onto the labor market exerts a downward pressure on wages, and the national minimum wage itself is too low to allow even a full-time worker to keep just herself and only one child above the official poverty line."

Poverty did decline under Clinton by almost 4 percentage

points. Yet, as Pollin explains, in the prosperity of the 1990s, this small drop back to 1974 levels is reprehensible: "Per capita GDP in 2000 was 70% higher than it was in 1974, productivity was 61% higher, and the stock market was up 603%."

Clinton's presidency did see a stop in wage decline from 1993 to 1996, however, according to Pollin. And in the next three years wages rose sharply. But "the real wage gains were also, in turn, largely a result of the stock market bubble. The Clinton economy of the late 1990s, whose successes were so heavily dependent on the stock market, offers little guidance as to what such an alternative path to sustained improvements in real wages might be.

"Moreover, conditions under Clinton worsened among those officially counted as poor. This is documented through data on the so called 'poverty gap,' which measures the amount of money needed to bring all poor people exactly up to the official poverty line. The poverty gap rose from $1,538 to $1,620 from 1993-99 (measured in 2001 dollars)."

Pollin continues, "Because workers had experienced the 'heightened sense of job insecurity' under most of Clinton's tenure, when wages did finally start to rise significantly in 1997, this was from an extremely low base. Moreover, the injection of increased spending under Clinton that produced low unemployment came from the stock market bubble, which, as has now become transparently clear, was unsustainable. In the 1960s, the catalyst driving the economy to full employment was government spending on the Vietnam War—that is, a source of economic stimulus that was also unsustainable and even more undesirable than the 1990s market bubble.

"The central challenge for an employment-targeted policy in the US today would therefore be to identify alternative sources of job expansion that do not require waging war or destabilizing the financial system. The Bush-2 plan for huge military spending increases obviously does not qualify any more than the Vietnam War as a desirable source of job expansion."

In other words, even though jobs were plentiful in the 1990s, poverty was widespread and, in fact, increasing. All this before the effects of NAFTA and welfare reform reared their ugly heads. But this was all by design. Clinton, et al., knew exactly what they were doing.

Quoting from Bob Woodward's *The Agenda*, Pollin reports that:

> Clinton himself acknowledged only weeks after winning the election that "We're Eisenhower Republicans here. We stand for lower deficits, free trade, and the bond market. Isn't that great?" Clinton further conceded during this same period that with his new policy focus "we help the bond market and we hurt the people who voted us in."

Would Kerry have reversed this trend? Not likely. Just as Bush did when he resurrected his father's economic team, Kerry promised to do the same with Clinton's old staff. During his campaign, key players of the Clinton squad—Roger C. Altman, Gene Sperling, and Sarah Bianchi, who worked for Al Gore in 2000—mapped out the Kerry economy. Ultimately, that economy proved to be nothing more than Clintonomics.

As Greg Bates, author of *Ralph's Revolt: The Case for Joining Nader's Rebellion*, argued during the campaign, "Kerry's economic policy shows the promise of moving the country rightward, just as Clinton's did. In fact, Kerry is running right so fast that he's running against the promises he made during the primaries."

Another example of Kerry's rightward push was his orientation toward the bond market. As the *Wall Street Journal* concluded in a May 3, 2004 article:

> Liberals worry that, in the White House, Mr. Kerry is

likely to tack even further toward the center. Some on the left complain Mr. Kerry is already doing so—undercutting the populism that was a key part of Mr. Clinton's 1992 campaign. 'The risk is that he's going to run the way Clinton governed, rather than the way Clinton ran,' says Robert Kuttner, editor of the liberal magazine *American Prospect.* 'No president ever got elected by promising to appease the bond market.'

"Kerry's advisors make clear where his presidency would take us," Bates reported. "As *The New York Times* headlined March 28, 2004, it's 'A Kerry Team, A Clinton Touch.' Four people are at the heart of the team. Roger C. Altman was a deputy Treasury secretary in the early Clinton years who got derailed by the Whitewater scandal and resigned. He's back, having invigorated his wallet with stock market wealth. The three other team members are Jason Furman, an economist trained at Harvard, Gene Sperling, who served under Clinton for all of the eight years, and Sarah Bianchi who served as Al Gore's health care specialist and later policy advisor during the 2000 campaign. And the man in the wings is Clinton's former Secretary of the Treasury. 'This group is consulting literally daily with Bob Rubin,' Altman told the *Times*."

"The right tax code will spark job creation at home," Sperling told the *Times*. "Gone was any whiff of aid for the poor, or any sense that government could reinvigorate the New Deal politics of FDR, which long ago sought to employ people directly instead of paying companies to do it indirectly—the latter being at greater cost to the taxpayer per job created and a far more dicey form of insuring the economic health of the country," wrote Bates.

It can be safely said that the economic pendulum would not have swung in the opposite direction had Kerry won the election. The number of people living in poverty would surely have increased. Jobs would still continue to be exported. Livelihoods would have continued to go down the drain. And health care for all would certainly not have been attainable, much less wished for by the Democrats.

"New spending must be offset by cuts in existing spending," *The New York Times* reported in the aforementioned report. Kerry made clear that spending on defense and Homeland Security would have continued to outpace inflation; the growth of these sectors would have imposed draconian fiscal discipline on the rest of the government if Kerry were to keep his pledge of balancing the federal budget.

The article also revealed what Kerry really meant by healthcare for all: not single-payer insurance, which is both the most widely favored and the most cost efficient and effective means for providing access to health care for all. Instead, money would have been shoveled to huge corporations: "Federal subsidies for some aspects of corporate health insurance," the *Times* reported. The May 3, 2004 edition of the *Wall Street Journal* quotes Kerry as saying of his health care subsidies, "I would think American businesses would jump up and down and welcome what I am offering."

Despite Kerry's campaign rhetoric, hope, we know, was *not* on the way. Continuing a sobering analysis of the two candidates just before the third debate on October 13, the *Wall Street Journal* reported:

> Mr. Kerry balances his support for new government programs with a Clintonian bow to limits on government action. His health care plan eschews regulatory mandates and is heavy on market-based incentives: It gives uninsured people tax credits to buy into existing plans and encourages companies to lower health care charges for employees by having the government subsidize their most expensive cases.

"Regulation of outsourcing is out the window, the only hope for actually addressing the more pernicious effects of globalization's race to find the cheapest worker," Bates wrote for Dissidentvoice.org in late October 2004. "Instead, Kerry will 'provide tax rebates to manufacturers that add jobs in the United States.' And he would cut corporate taxes—already at astonishing low levels—by 5%. It could be a nice tax break—offset in part by forcing companies with overseas income to pay tax on it immediately instead of deferring it indefinitely. Then, to cut the deficit by $250 billion, Kerry will reinstate the tax rates Bush cut on those households earning over $200,000 a year. Sounds good, but there is no plan to cut back on Bush's bloated defense and Homeland Security spending."

The comparisons you've read thus far, be it economics or war, show just how the Republicans have taken advantaged of liberal follies. The Democrats continually ignore and neglect their traditional base: For they are supposed to be the party of the people—the minorities, the poor, and all those who do not have a political voice.

Chapter Thirteen

On Civil Liberties Myopia

Bush Didn't Start the war on the Bill of Rights

with Merlin Chowkwanyun

"During the Clinton administration, the Department of Justice grew faster than any other agency of the federal government."

The Washington Post, February 9, 2001

The Democrats have not only waged a war on the poor. They have also waged a war on the Bill of Rights. When did the assault on Americans' civil liberties get jumpstarted? The current liberal establishment seems to deem the 9/11 terrorist attacks the chief catalyst. Many within this club imply that drastic incursions on Americans' civil liberties only began after 9/11, while the Clinton administration represented a civil liberties paradise.

Take, for instance, John Kerry supporter and stand-up comedian Margaret Cho, who at a MoveOn benefit railed: "I mean, I'm afraid of terrorism, but I'm more afraid of the Patriot Act," even though her candidate of choice not only voted for the legislation but authored many of its components.

Or how about Al Gore, who in 2003 exclaimed: "They have taken us much farther down the road toward an intrusive, Big Brother-style government—toward the dangers prophesied by George Orwell in his book *1984*—than anyone ever thought would be possible in the United States of America."

With such a sour musk in the air, it is not surprising that hysteria reigned supreme over how much George W. Bush's administration was to blame for the police conduct at the

Republican National Convention in the summer of 2004, when more than a thousand protestors were detained for up to 50 hours prior to being released. This infringement was indeed awful—but hardly unique to the Bush years alone.

In early 2002, for instance, more than 20 FBI agents raided the home of Southern California African-American anarchist Sherman Austin's mother and seized her son's computers, which he used to run a political website.

"They showed me a search warrant, and I just glanced at it … They just went into the house. They searched all the rooms in the house. They knew where my room was. They went back there, looked at all the computers, asked me to come in and tell them what all the computers were for specifically so they knew how to dismantle the network I had been running," Austin recalled. "They searched the garage, pretty much everywhere with their guns still out and drawn. They still had people surrounding the house with their weapons drawn."

Austin was later charged and sentenced to a year in prison for "distribution" of information about making or using explosives with the "intent" that the information "be used for, or in furtherance of, an activity that constitutes a Federal crime of violence."

Austin did not author the information, which was housed on a section of the site he allocated to a teenager who then proceeded to upload the instructions. Rather, Austin provided activists with free web space, where they could upload their own web pages at will.

"They said I was being arrested for distribution of information related to explosives over the Internet," says Austin. "My site was linked to another site, which wasn't affiliated with raisethefist.com, but which was hosted on the same server because I gave hosting space to different people who wanted some free hosting. I just provided the link to that site. It was called the *Reclaim Guide*. It was just a general protest guide that went over security culture and stuff like that. A small portion of that guide dealt with explosives information. This information was just pathetic compared to the type of stuff you could find in any library or any other website ... There's something on the Internet called the *White Resistance Manual*. It's pretty much for white supremacists ... to carry out a large-scale guerilla campaign through means of assassination, threats, obtaining funds through fraud, everything from firearms to explosives. I've seen, not surprisingly, no action taken against those people, but here I am, an anarchist website, not even close to what that is, not even close to what else you can find on the Internet."

The obscure federal statute used against Austin, and which carried many implications for free speech, hit the books in the late 1990s, long before Bush, with the legislative shepherding of Democratic Senator Dianne Feinstein of California. Sadly, liberal publications like the *American Prospect* and *The Nation* said nothing of Austin's case.

"The statute that Senator Dianne Feinstein sponsored and wrote just goes to show that this has been happening for a while," claims Austin.

Indeed, Austin is correct.

During the 2000 Republican National Convention in Philadelphia, police arrested Ruckus Society founder John Sellers for walking down the street. Police brutality easily exceeded anything seen at the New York City Republican National Convention at the 2000 Democratic National Convention in LA, where an outdoor Rage Against the Machine concert came to an abrupt end after riot police fired rubber bullets and tear gas at protestors and many non-participating bystanders, including media personnel.

Journalist and consumer advocate Dave Horowitz, who attended the Democratic National Convention in 2000, wandered into trouble while carrying a video camera and audio gear after a tiresome day of interviewing delegates at the event. "It was his bad luck to arrive … just as protesters and concertgoers were trying to leave," as John Seeley reported in the *LA Weekly* on August 25, 2000. "He ran to what he thought was a safe spot and pulled out a small digital video camera to record the action."

Seeley continued:

> As Horowitz recounts events on his *www.fightback. com* Web site, though his press pass was clearly visible, an officer "came at me with a baton, and shouted, 'Move! Move, or else!' I turned, and another officer swung at me with his baton, while the second officer knocked me down and kicked the camera out of my hand. I shouted, 'I'm press, I'm press! Please stop!' Then a third officer kicked my briefcase into a nearby wall as rubber-bullet shots crackled like firecrackers around me."

It was almost three hours before Horowitz was readmitted to the area to recover the briefcase. While his day's notes were still inside, his 35mm camera and the shot roll of film it contained were missing. Horowitz, who describes his long relationship with the LAPD as excellent, found its Monday night actions a shock: "The police attacked the crowd with such ferocity that it reminded me of disturbances I covered in wartime Saigon, where demonstrators were shot by overzealous police trying to control the crowd and their public image."

Going back a bit further to 1999, during the WTO protests in Seattle, riot police beat up marchers, sprayed tear gas, and shot rubber bullets indiscriminately. Protestors were locked out of several downtown blocks and public parks, where individuals could not even wear anti-WTO paraphernalia.

As journalist Jeffrey St. Clair wrote in *Five Days That Shook the World*:

> Tear gas canisters were unloaded and then five or six of them were fired into the crowd. One of the protesters

nearest the cops was a young, petite woman. She rose up, obviously disoriented from the gas, and a Seattle policeman, crouched less than 10 feet away, shot her in the knee with a rubber bullet. She fell to the pavement, grabbing her leg and screaming in pain. Then, moments later, one of her comrades, maddened by the unprovoked attack, charged the police line, Kamikaze-style. Two cops beat him to the ground with their batons, hitting him at least 20 times.

At the regional level, a May Day 2001 march in Long Beach, California, ended similarly, with many activists having to enter the emergency room because of wounds inflicted by police officers, some of which left rubber bullets lodged under skins. May Day protesters amassing in Portland, Oregon in 2000 experienced similar acts when police violently corralled activists, forcing them to retreat for fear of being stampeded by mounted police horses.

Then there's the racist and institutionalized police state that existed throughout the 1980s but really took new hold during the 1990s with the Clinton era spike in so-called "War on Drugs" activity, which has led to the record incarceration of African-Americans, Latinos, and women.

"Although Republicans are normally thought to hold the tough on crime mantle, in President Clinton's first-term (1992-1996), 148,000 more state and federal prisoners were added than under President Reagan's first term (1980-1984), and 34,000 more than were added under President Bush's four-year term (1988-1992)," stated the Center on Juvenile and Criminal Justice in a 2001 report titled "Too Little Too Late: President Clinton's Prison Legacy."

The report contended:

> When President Bill Clinton included "the war on crime" as a major tenet in both his 1992 and 1996 presidential campaigns, the past ten years had already witnessed the largest incarceration increase in the nation's history. During

his 1992 campaign, to illustrate his resolve, President Clinton actually interrupted his campaigning to return to his home state of Arkansas to oversee the execution of mentally retarded death row inmate Ricky Ray Rector.

Throughout its tenure, the Clinton administration consistently supported increased penalties and additional prison construction. The Violent Crime Control and Law Enforcement Act of 1994 provided state and municipal governments with $30 billion to add 100,000 new police officers, to build more prisons, and to employ more prison guards, as well as funding for crime prevention programs.

Fraternities have also long existed in major metropolitan police departments, wherein members ascend the ranks for beatings, flouting guidelines, and planting evidence. When one individual instance of this was exposed, as happened when police officers in LA's Ramparts division were found to have planted drug evidence, commentators preferred to describe it as a slight blight on an otherwise functioning system. In actuality, this so called "blight" represented an extremity of the norm.

Racist profiling, harassment of black and Latino youth under the guise of "anti-gang" activity, and no-knock SWAT raids on the homes of non-whites supposedly in possession of drugs or illegal weapons increased dramatically under Bill Clinton.

In fact, what we are seeing today is a logical continuation of a foundation laid during the Clinton era. Before the now well-known Patriot Act there was the unknown Antiterrorism and Effective Death Penalty Act, signed into law following the Oklahoma City bombing that took place on August 19, 1995, and which prompted the worst assaults on civil liberties the United States had seen in decades.

"Members of Congress immediately felt tremendous pressure to pass antiterrorism legislation," legal scholars David Cole and James Dempsey write in *Terrorism and the Constitution*.

"It did not matter that the proposals in the President's initial bill were directed largely against international terrorism, while the Oklahoma bombing was the work of homegrown discontents ... Eager to get the bill on the President's desk by the April 19 anniversary of the Oklahoma City bombing, the Senate adopted the conference report on April 17 in a 91-8 vote. The next day, the House also adopted the report by a vote of 293-133. On April 24, President Clinton signed The Antiterrorism and Effective Death Penalty Act of 1996."

"To make the death penalty effective," explains civil liberties expert Elaine Cassel in *The War on Civil Liberties*, "meant making it harder to appeal convictions of capital offenses." Clinton's law, says Cassel, also "[made] it a crime to support even the lawful activities of an organization labeled as terrorist ... [authorized] the FBI to investigate the crime of 'material support' for terrorism based solely on activities protected under the First Amendment ... [freezes] assets of any US citizen or domestic organization believed to be an agent of a terrorist group, without specifying an 'agent' ... [expanded] the powers of the secret court ... [repealed] the law that barred the FBI from opening investigations based solely on activities protected under the First Amendment ... [and allowed] the Immigration and Naturalization Service (now called the US Citizenship and Immigration Services) to deport citizens (mostly Muslims) upon the order of INS officials."

Of course, these are but a few of the ways in which the Clinton administration infringed upon civil liberties. Clinton himself admitted to making "a number of ill-advised changes in our immigration laws, having nothing to do with fighting terrorism."

In the wake of September 11, Clinton's successor, along with Attorney General John Ashcroft, perhaps not so surprisingly, legislated additional infringements upon civil liberties in the name of patriotism and national security.

Spun as such, the legislation enjoyed overwhelming support,

so much so that Democratic Senator Russell Feingold of Wisconsin, one of a handful of Democrats who reached across the aisle to confirm Ashcroft following the tremulous 2000 election—was the only member of the Senate to vote against the legislation.

Nevertheless, the liberal myopia was, and still is, astounding.

Michael Moore, hero of the liberal establishment and uninformed "activists" who view Bush-bashing as social glue, claims to have read the Patriot Act in his award-winning film *Fahrenheit 9/11*. However, the two cases he cites in the film's segment on the Patriot Act have absolutely nothing to do with the legislation. Local law enforcement's infiltration of activist groups (Moore's first case) and law enforcement's questioning of the politically outspoken (case two) occurred during the 1990s, particularly after the WTO protests.

For foreigners and immigrants on American soil, as well as the Guantánamo prisoners in Cuba, all egregiously skipped over in Moore's movie, post-9/11 legal changes have resulted in sweeping rights to detain, torture, and harass. But this is not something that entirely rests with Bush, Jr., alone. In actuality, the Democrats ushered in the legislation that made Bush's more egregious intrusions possible.

The Democrats hardly have made it an issue since then and have instead gone ahead and condoned the appointment of Bush's "torture memos" guru Alberto Gonzales to replace John Ashcroft as Attorney General.

On January 6, 2005, the *Minneapolis Star Tribune* criticized the Gonzales nomination:

> At the height of the Abu Ghraib scandal, someone leaked to *Newsweek* a memorandum Gonzales authored in January 2002, which argued that the war on terror had "rendered obsolete" the Geneva Conventions prohibiting torture and abuse of prisoners of war. The conventions,

he said, did not apply to enemy combatants captured in Afghanistan. Gonzales also was a principal architect of Bush's order authorizing the secret trial of combatants from Afghanistan by military tribunal.

Only within the last few days has it become known just how key a role Gonzales played in the formation of a notorious Department of Justice memo issued in August 2002. That memo defined torture quite narrowly—it said that only physical pain "of an intensity akin to that which accompanies serious physical injury such as death or organ failure" amounted to torture. It also said the president had inherent authority to authorize use of extreme means of interrogation on detainees suspected of terrorist activities.

Still the ACLU would not "take an official position." Pro-war Democrat Charles Schumer opined: "It's encouraging that the President has chosen someone less polarizing [than Ashcroft]." And Patrick Leahy, ranking Senate Democrat of Vermont who sits on the Senate Judiciary Committee, chimed in tellingly: "I like him."

In short, by ascribing all the civil liberties tribulations of this country to one date, September 11, 2001, and one administration, George W. Bush's, the liberal establishment has avoided any painstaking analysis of our systemic civil liberties problems that would indeed point back in its own members' direction. Like so many other issues, the Democrats had been doing Bush's work for him all along.

For those interested in helping or learning more about Sherman Austin's ongoing case, please visit www.freesherman.org

Chapter Fourteen

Forging Alliances

How Democrats Helped Bush Destroy Mother Nature

George W. Bush's environmental record can be summed up in one simple word: devastating.

Not only has President Bush gutted numerous environmental laws—including the Clean Air and Water Acts—he has also set a new precedent by disregarding the world's top scientists and the Pentagon, whose concerns about the rate of global warming grow graver by the day. This by no means implies that John Kerry is significantly different, but we'll get to that in a moment.

As Mark Townsend and Paul Harris reported for the *UK Observer* in February 2004, "[The Pentagon report] predicts that abrupt climate change could bring the planet to the edge of anarchy as countries develop a nuclear threat to defend and secure dwindling food, water, and energy supplies. The threat to global stability vastly eclipses that of terrorism, say the few experts privy to its contents."

Bush's Environmental Protection Agency (EPA) even admits that climate change is being exacerbated by Americans' consumptive culture. "What has changed in the last few hundred years is the additional release of carbon dioxide by human activities," the EPA admits. "Fossil fuels burned to run cars and trucks, heat homes and businesses, and power factories are responsible for about 98% of US carbon dioxide emissions, 24% of methane emissions, and 18% of nitrous oxide emissions. Increased agriculture, deforestation, landfills, industrial production, and mining also contribute a significant share of emissions. In 1997, the United States emitted about one-fifth of total global greenhouse gases."

It was easy for Bush to back out of the Kyoto Protocol when Al Gore and Bill Clinton undermined the agreement in the late nineties. "Signing the Protocol, while an important step forward, imposes no obligations on the United States. The Protocol becomes binding only with the advice and consent of the US Senate," Gore said at the time. "As we have said before, we will not submit the Protocol for ratification without the meaningful participation of key developing countries in efforts to address climate change." And Gore stood by his promise.

Although Kyoto was a gigantic step forward in addressing global warming, the Democratic Party collectively opposed the watered down version of the Protocol. They did so to avoid alienating their labor base, which worried that new environmental laws would shift jobs to developing nations with weaker environmental regulations. Hence Kyoto's derailment and the Democrats failed challenge to Bush's misdeeds.

Grim Appointments

Around the same time that Bush crushed Kyoto, he nominated Gale Norton to be his Secretary of the Interior, a position which oversees approximately one-fifth of all US land. "As Colorado's attorney general in the mid '90s, she chalked up a scandalous record: looking the other way in the face of damaging pollution, dragging her feet on prosecuting big business, even challenging the Environmental Protection Agency's authority to override state law," James Ridgeway wrote for *The Village Voice* in February 2001. "When a gold mine spilled cyanide into a local river, killing all aquatic life along a 17-mile stretch, Norton declined to press criminal charges and stalled so badly the feds stepped in. In another spectacular case, she testified against her own citizens, siding with a big corporation that fouled the air.

"Norton was trained for the role as interior secretary in the saber-rattling libertarian wing of the Republican Party. She climbed the ladder from former interior chief James Watts' Mountain States Legal Foundation through the Hoover Institution to the Reagan administration. Back in Colorado, she immersed herself in pure libertarian politics at the Political Economy Research Center. Along the way, she became ensconced in the property rights network, from the Sagebrush Rebellion of the Reagan era to today's militant Wise Use Movement and the rock-ribbed Defenders of Property Rights."

And yet the majority of Senate Democrats, including Tom Daschle of South Dakota, Robert Byrd of West Virginia, and California's Dianne Feinstein, supported Norton's grim appointment despite their power to obstruct her confirmation.

Dirty Energy

With that kind of opposition, it is little wonder why Bush had no qualms about moving forward with his dirty energy plan, which became known as the "Energy Policy Act of 2003." Bush's bill called for a slash in renewable energy funding and an increase in fossil fuel consumption. The bill, authored by Vice President Cheney's Energy Task Force, met with a reported 39 oil lobbyists and executives to draft the legislation.

Joan Claybrook, president of the consumer rights watchdog group Public Citizen, wrote of Enron's corrupt involvement in the writing of the bill:

> [Enron] was one of the most aggressive proponents of natural gas and electricity deregulation and was the most influential player in developing Bush's energy policy. Sorting out this tangled web of political influence, greed, deceit, and corporate hubris will take hundreds of lawyers, dozens of congressional committee hearings, and multiple investigations

by law enforcement agencies … Vice President Dick Cheney met privately with Lay to discuss the formulation of the administration's energy plan, from which Lay stood to benefit enormously. The Bush administration has refused to release the records of the meeting and other deliberations of its energy task force, even in the face of congressional demands.

Over 30 Democrats in the House of Representatives voted in favor of Bush's legislation, while eight others decided not to cast a vote on the measure, which ultimately passed effortlessly through the House. The Senate Democrats stepped up their opposition, halting the bill. Ultimately, they came back with a horrid version of their own, which 36 Democrats, including ranking leaders such as Senator Tom Daschle, Iowa Senator Tom Harkin, and John Edwards of North Carolina, voted for.

Offering few variations from the Task Force's original draft, the Democratic version set aside almost $2 billion for big coal companies and $1 billion in tax breaks for nuclear power expansion in addition to over $5 billion in hand-outs and tax cuts for the oil industry.

The bill also earmarked over $20 billion for the building of an oil pipeline from Alaska to the lower 48 states. And as Ted Virdone and Jyo Bhatt reported for the *Socialist Alternative* during the bill's development in 2002:

> The pipeline will be privately owned and operated, so although the costs would be socialized, the profits are privatized. The bill also eliminates many vehicle safety regulations.
>
> Democrats say that the Senate bill is environmentally friendly because it requires new cars to get 35 miles per gallon by 2013, and it requires that renewable energy comprise 10% of all retail electricity by 2020 … The technology already exists for *all* passenger vehicles to achieve that gas mileage, but the auto industry has refused to utilize that technology for

new SUVs and trucks, and Congress has passed moratoriums on new fuel efficiency research.

The Heritage Foundation, a neoconservative-laden right-wing think tank based in Washington, DC, boasted of the Democrats' rewrite: "[The] bill includes provisions that strengthen the nation's electricity system and, at the margins, narrows the gap between supply and demand. There are **no**: Mandatory renewable portfolio standards; Climate change initiatives; Statutory increases in corporate average fuel economy (CAFE) standards; and Mandatory regional transmission organizations (RTOs)."

The Strip Club

Like his predecessors Bill Clinton and Al Gore, President Bush saw nothing wrong with the disastrous practice of hilltop strip mining (mountain-top removal) and overturned a federal ruling that had banned the practice during the Clinton years, despite the dismay of Al Gore. The push to lift the ban came from the stubborn Steven Griles, a scion of the mining industry and Interior Secretary Gale Norton's top advisor in Washington. Democrats again offered little in the way of opposition, as they have historically backed the disastrous mining practice.

On May 13, 2002, the Ohio Valley Environmental Coalition issued a plea for opposition to the strip mine ruling. "In mountaintop removal coal companies blast off the tops of mountains to mine thin seams of coal. Rubble from the former mountaintops is pushed into 'valley fills,' burying streams in nearby valleys under hundreds of millions of tons of mining waste. In West Virginia alone, over 1,000 miles of streams have been obliterated by valley fills."

Then in another bold move, the Bush administration pandered to corporate timber barons and authored a new anti-forest plan—ironically entitled the "Healthy Forests Initiative"—which mirrored Clinton's chainsaw-happy Salvage Rider Act of 1995. Democratic senators, including Oregon's Ron Wyden and California's Dianne Feinstein, eventually rewrote Bush's legislation. It was little surprise that Wyden supported the corporate timber bill, for no other senator receives more loot from the timber industry than Oregon's Wyden.

Logging without Laws

The Clinton administration's Salvage Rider, known to radical environmentalists as the "Logging without Laws" rider, was perhaps the most gruesome legislation ever enacted under the pretext of preserving ecosystem health. Like the Bush-Wyden-Feinstein forest initiative, Clinton's act was choc full of deception and special interest pandering.

"When [the Salvage Rider] bill was given to me, I was told that the timber industry was circulating this language among the Northwest Congressional delegation and others to try to get it attached as a rider to the fiscal year Interior Spending Bill," environmental lawyer Kevin Kirchner says. "There is no question that representatives of the timber industry had a role in promoting this rider. That is no secret."

In fact, Mark Rey, a former lobbyist for the timber industry and head of the United States Forest Service under Bush, authored the "Healthy Forest" plan and Clinton's salvage bill while working as an aide for Republican Senator Larry Craig of Idaho. "Like Bush's so-called 'Healthy Forest Initiative,' the Salvage Rider temporarily exempted salvage timber sales on federal forest lands from environmental and wildlife laws, administrative appeals, and judicial review," contends the Wilderness Society.

"The Salvage Rider directed the Forest Service to cut old-growth timber in the Pacific Northwest that the agency had proposed for sale but subsequently withdrew due to environmental concerns, endangered species listings, and court rulings. Bush's initiative also aims to increase logging of old-growth trees in the Pacific Northwest."

Clinton during the time could have exercised presidential authority to force the relevant agencies to abandon all timber contracts that stemmed from the Salvage Rider. But he never flexed his muscle and instead sat by as the forests were subjected to gruesome annihilation.

Thousands of acres of healthy forestland across the West were rampaged. Washington's Colville National Forest saw the clear cutting of over 4,000 acres. Thousands more in Montana's Yaak River Basin, hundreds of acres of pristine forest land in Idaho, while the endangered Mexican Spotted Owl habitat in Arizona fell victim to corporate interests. Old growth trees in Washington's majestic Olympic Peninsula—home to wild Steelhead, endangered Sockeye salmon, and threatened Marbled Murrelet—were chopped with unremitting provocation by the US Forest Service. And the assault on nature continued with Clinton's blessing.

Just before Bush announced his version of Clinton's salvage law, Democratic Senator Tom Daschle beat him to the punch, slipping his own crass language into a defense appropriations bill in the summer of 2002. Daschle's legal jargon, backed by the Sierra Club and the Wilderness Society, allowed unharnessed logging on American Indian land in his home state of South Dakota. These very holy lands, which the Sioux call *Paha Sapa*, were once a visionary refuge for Lakota elders, including Crazy Horse and Black Elk.

As Jeffrey St. Clair wrote, "[The plan will allow] timber companies to begin logging in the Beaver Park roadless area and in the Norbeck Wildlife Preserve. These two areas harbor some of the last remaining stands of old-growth forest in the Black Hills. All of these timber sales will be shielded from environmental lawsuits, even from organizations that objected to the deal … The logging plan was consecrated in the name of fire prevention. The goal of the bill, Daschle said, 'is to reduce the risk of forest fire by getting [logging] crews on the ground as quickly as possible to start thinning.' It's long been the self-serving contention of the timber lobby that the only way to prevent forest fires is to log them first."

A product of Clinton and Daschle's cunning style, Bush's own forest plan—supported by the overwhelming majority of Democrats in the Senate—authorized the use of over $760 million in hopes of preventing wild fires. The legislation, renamed the "Healthy Forests Restoration Act," accomplishes no such thing, of course. Instead, the bill sanctions the pillage of over 2.5 million acres of Federal forest land by 2012, including the single largest US Forest Service timber sale in modern history, where 30 square miles of Federal lands in Oregon, named the "Biscuit Fire Recovery Project," could be logged, despite over 23,000 public statements denouncing the proposal.

With only thirteen casting a "no" vote on the grisly legislation, Democrats folded big time, backing the bill they should have been working tooth-and-nail to defeat. Incidentally, John Kerry forgot to show up for work that day and never voted.

Although the Democrats caved to Bush's demands, some environmentalists claim that Clinton's policies have been more detrimental to US forests than Bush's. Of course you'll never hear this from any mainstream environmental group. As veteran forest activist Michael Donnelly of Salem, Oregon, wrote in *CounterPunch* in December 2003:

> Perhaps the greatest irony is that the forests have fared far better under Bush than they did under his Democrat predecessor. Under Clinton's [Salvage Rider] plan, some 1.1 billion board feet of Ancient Forest stumps were authorized annually. Much to the industry's chagrin, under Bush, around 200 million per year has been cut. Already, that means that

2.7 billion board feet LESS has been cut under Bush than would have been under a Gore administration with the Big Greens' usual silence regarding Democrat stump-creation.

And if Bush were to continue at this rate for a total of eight years, then the "total cut of Ancient Forests will be 1.6 billion board feet, exactly what was cut in just one year under Clinton's 1995 'Salvage Rider,' Donnelly contends.

Bush followed his forest follies by pushing his Clear Skies initiative, which calls for a reduction in the limit of harsh chemicals industrial polluters are permitted to emit.

Although this plan hasn't been written into legislation, Bush currently aims to cut the US's "carbon intensity" by measuring the harsh pollutants with an economic model, rather than a scientific analysis. "The President is giving Congress an opportunity to deal with a key environmental and public health challenge—but only if the legislation it enacts is significantly stronger than the President's proposal," explains Joseph Goffman, a senior attorney for Environmental Defense. "The Environmental Protection Agency's own air quality modeling and economic analyses show that deeper pollution reductions than called for under CSI are cost-effective and absolutely necessary to protect public health and the environment. CSI calls for reductions in sulfur dioxide ($SO2$), oxides of nitrogen (NO), and mercury, but none in carbon dioxide pollution."

The Republicans' proposed 2005 budget—which has the support of many Senate Democrats—calls for almost $2 billion in cuts for environmental protection, including $500 million in cuts from the states' Clean Water Fund. And on July 13, 2004, the Bush administration moved to roll back a road-less logging rule that was enacted in the waning days of the Clinton/Gore era. Clinton's nature-friendly move was a token gesture to the environmental community, which protected 58.5 million acres of wilderness area from new road development.

However, Clinton's effort was simply an election year stunt aimed at courting the green vote that was fleeing into Ralph Nader's camp at a substantial rate in 2000. But astute environmental activists knew the clever protection wouldn't last for long. Any protection initiated by executive order can be dismantled the same way. So when Bush's announcement to kill Clinton's decree came a day after he called for a possible postponement of the 2004 election in case of a terror attack, it was no big surprise. The decision will open these areas to road development, and eventually mass logging and oil procurement, if state governors fail to petition the initiatives. Time will tell whether Democratic governors will stand up for the rights of our national forests and federal wilderness areas. But don't count on it. Their record isn't much better than their wretched opposition.

In some aspects the Democrats may be marginally better than the Republicans. At least they believe in evolution, and most likely don't get their science lessons from the Old Testament.

A slight variation in beliefs won't win elections, however; it's policy on the ground that matters. And the Democrats have not offered a substantial alternative to the Republican agenda regarding the environment. John Kerry, and the party whose shoulders on which he stands was determined not to rock the boat, which is one of the reasons why George W. Bush remains "leader of the free world."

Chapter Fifteen

The Lost Club

Environmental Group on the Verge of Extinction

Earth Day came and went as usual in 2004, with the renewed hope that our elected politicians and conservationists are indeed concerned with our planet's environmental welfare. George W. Bush boastfully exclaimed that his administration, if reelected, "will expand the wetlands of America." And his presidential opponent, John Kerry, claimed to be "greener" than Bush and declared that, unlike GW, he would not allow environmental legislation to be "written by polluters in exchange for campaign contributions."

Unfortunately, reality paints another picture: Earth Day has morphed into the Valentine's Day of the corporate environmental movement. April 22 has become the token feel-good holiday for oily politicians and corporate conservationists—a day to tout their commitment and affection for the natural world.

It's no wonder then that Carl Pope, director of the Sierra Club and the poster boy for the suited conservation movement, used Earth Day to release his book, *Strategic Ignorance: Why the Bush Administration is Recklessly Destroying a Century of Environmental Progress*. In his not-so-seminal manuscript Pope writes, "This is what the American people do not know: The Bush administration is full of officials who believe—from the bottom of their hearts, not just their wallets—that weaker laws on clean air, less funding to clean up toxic waste dumps, and national parks and forests run for private profit are actually good for the country."

Pope only has it half right. Bush is bad, no doubt. But in reality, compromising mainstream organizations like his own Sierra Club have enabled Republicans and their Democratic brethren to roll back a century's worth of environmental progress.

Here is a small-scale example, of which there are many.

Wisconsin's Clean Water Action Council had its own battle with Club Sierra in the summer of 2003. The conflict ensued over the "government's plan to unnecessarily allow significant public health risks to persist on the Fox River" near Green Bay. Clean Water Action Council contended that it had "consistently [stated] over two years that the sediments must be removed down to .25 ppm PCBs in order to reach average PCB levels low enough to eliminate the need for fish consumption warnings."

"However," the group contended, "the government has chosen to dredge down to 1 ppm PCBs, a level which is 90 times higher than PCB sediment concentrations that are fully protective of human health. [This] policy will leave a large mass of PCBs behind in the river, which will continue to bleed toxic contamination for many decades into the future. Roughly 40,000 people are currently eating unsafe quantities of fish from the Fox River and Green Bay. We must take action to protect these people and future generations."

Despite Fox River Watch's dedicated efforts to clean up the local stream, the Sierra Club undermined many months worth of discussions. In a statement released following the EPA's announcement, the Sierra Club stated, "[T]he fundamental cleanup plan is solid … [and] We applaud the EPA [for] developing a protective cleanup plan that is based on good science."

The Clean Water Action Council was less than thrilled. "The odd thing about the Sierra Club's news releases is that they are inconsistent with the Sierra Club's own position on the clean up standard," the Council wrote following the saga. "Many times over the past 2 years, the Sierra Club has advocated for the same .25 ppm PCB cleanup target that we support. Their testimony at the public hearings, their formal written comments to the agencies, and their action alerts for their members—all promoted the .25 ppm standard ... they should be helping us. Instead, the Sierra Club is squandering its resources and actively working against the local citizens along the Fox River and Green Bay who are most damaged by the PCB contamination."

Following the brokered deal, several Sierra Club chapters, frustrated at how the Club representatives caved on their own commitments, wrote letters to the EPA denouncing the agreement. But it was too little too late; the Sierra Club had already compromised their integrity.

This story is hardly an isolated incident. Time and time again, the Sierra Club's leadership has undermined grassroots efforts by flexing their negotiating muscle and compromising positions at crunch time.

Blazing it up in Big Sky Country

Still skeptical? Consider this:

Following the historic blazes in Montana's Bitterroot Mountains during the blistering summer of 2000, many looking to turn a quick buck embraced the government's outlandish position that clear-cutting the forest reduces the risk of fire. And on cue, the obliging forest service mapped out over 46,000 acres of land that were ripe for the mulling. Along with numerous other environmental organizations, including American Wildlands and the Ecological Center, the Sierra Club, trusty liberals that they are, initially opposed the deal.

The lawsuit was sent all the way to the Ninth Circuit Court of Appeals in San Francisco before returning back to federal Judge Don Molloy in Montana. By then, the Sierra Club was primed for compromise. As Jeffrey St. Clair reported in March 2002, Sierra Club president Jennifer Ferenstein "faxed a settlement proposal to the Bush administration that included a concession that would allow areas to be logged within days. 'The signal we gave is that we are willing to consider an option that put people [i.e. loggers] out on the ground ... We can be flexible.'"

Montana Senator Max Baucus (yeah, him again) weighed in and called for a quick resolution that would allow certain sales to proceed. "The opposing sides convened for a two-day session in Missoula," St. Clair reported. "And the deal was hatched. It calls for 60 million board feet of timber sales and clear-cutting on about 14,000 acres of land. The enviros signed away the right to challenge those sales, regardless of their environmental consequences ... So 60 million board feet of clearcuts are sanctioned without regard to their damage to an already stressed ecosystem. The enviros involved have tried to downplay the damage these clearcuts will cause. But think of it this way: it will still represent one of the largest timber sales in Montana history. The sale volume is four times what the entire Bitterroot forest has been logging per year for the past decade."

Such heartbreaking concessions gave birth to Earth First! in 1979, when the irritation and loathing of a few radical environmentalists, including Dave Foreman and Mike Roselle (now with the Ruckus Society), prompted them to form an unyielding organization to counter enviro stooges like the behemoth Club.

Regrettably, the Sierra Club never reverted back to its radical John Muir roots, instead becoming even more skilled at cutting deals under the guise of stewardship. And the Club can certainly be accused of chronic lying when it promises its 600,000-plus members, "When you join or give to the Sierra Club, you will have the satisfaction of knowing that you are helping to preserve irreplaceable wildlands, save endangered and threatened wildlife, and protect this fragile environment we call home." In actuality, the only thing you can be sure of is that Carl Pope and other Sierra Club executives will do their best to guard their lofty six-figure salaries to the detriment of the environment.

Compromise This!

Well before the aforementioned illustrations, David Brower, founder of the Earth Island Institute, Friends of the Earth, and the first executive director of the Sierra Club, wrote Doug Scott, acting conservation director of the Club in 1989, about the role of dreadful "compromise" within the organization:

> My thesis is that compromise is often necessary but that it ought not originate with the Sierra Club. We are to hold fast to what we believe is right, fight for it, and find allies and adduce all possible arguments for our cause. If we cannot find enough vigor in us or them to win, then let someone else propose the compromise. We thereupon work hard to coax it our way. We become a nucleus around which the strongest force can build and function.
>
> The Sierra Club compromised enough to lose its best antinuclear group. The Club has compromised enough to be of little force or effect in slowing the arms race. The Club was asked to act four years ago [on] environmental concerns in Nicaragua, but has remained silent. The Club backed away from saving the California condor in the wild. The Club did not join in the fight to block the new San Onofre reactors (a failure of which, quite possibly, could make Southern California uninhabitable). The Club so misjudges the arms race that it discourages the San Diego chapter from protesting in Nevada, as if such a global problem must be left exclusively to the Toiyabe chapter. The national club, and Sierra Club California, seem to think that the inexcusable charring of giant sequoias in Sequoia National Park and the terminal isolation of giant sequoias of Sequoia National Forest, and the monocultural new plantations being planted around them is the province of the Kern-Kaweah chapter and severe damage continues. The Club thinks that stopping the charring of sequoias in Yosemite is the business of the Tehipite chapter, and the damage continues ... The Club is

so eager to appear reasonable that it goes soft, undercuts the strong grassroots efforts of chapters, groups, and other organizations.

And now we have pompous liberals like Pope and Kerry who refuse to accept any culpability for environmental disasters, instead blaming their exacerbation on the Bush administration. But in fact it is compromises by each of these men's respective clubs that have precluded protection of the wild.

Spanking the Donkey

In 1996, 2000, and 2004, the Sierra Club failed to endorse presidential candidate Ralph Nader even though his campaign clearly mirrored the Club's official positions more closely than those of Clinton, Gore, or Kerry.

In October 1996, the "Draft Nader for President" Clearinghouse released a statement denouncing the Club and its endorsement of Bill Clinton:

> From the opening hours of the administration began the retreat from the high-minded environmental promises of the '92 campaign … First there was the WTI hazardous waste incinerator located outside East Liverpool, Ohio, which Al Gore had promised repeatedly to shut down. Within weeks of taking office, operating permits were issued. This was followed by Interior Secretary Bruce Babbitt's destructive deal with the sugar barons of South Florida, dooming vast acreages of the Everglades. Then the administration capitulated to the demands of Western Democrats and yanked from its initial budget proposals to reform grazing, mining, and timber practices on federal lands. In April, Clinton convened a Timber summit in Portland, Oregon, dominated by logging interests; the predictable outcome of this session was a plan to restart clear-cutting in the ancient forests of the Pacific Northwest for the first time in three years. Then the

administration pulled out every stop to secure the passage of the North American Free Trade Agreement (NAFTA), which has been an unprecedented environmental disaster on both sides of the border. They repeated the mistake a year later by pushing through an updated version of the General Agreement on Tariffs and Trade (GATT), which gave the World Trade Organization (WTO) the ability to strike down American environmental laws.

In July of '95 the administration dealt its heaviest blow to the American environment by signing the so-called Salvage Logging Rider, a bill which suspended the application of all environmental laws governing federal forests. And on the eve of the Democratic convention, President Clinton gave the food and chemical industries a victory they had sought for 40 years when he signed a bill striking down the Delaney clause, a law that prohibited the addition of carcinogens to processed foods. This presidential action is the environment equivalent of signing the welfare bill. In each of these instances, the Sierra Club had an official position in opposition to the actions taken by the administration. But the Sierra Club's recent endorsement of the Clinton/Gore administration mentions none of these egregious actions.

The Club begged to differ with the Draft Nader campaign. "Bill Clinton and Al Gore have demonstrated a strong commitment to protecting America's environment, for our families and our future," the Club insisted. And in 2000, Pope, responding to Nader's plea for the Sierra Club's endorsement, wrote, "You [Nader] have called upon us to vote our hopes, not our fears. I find it easy to do so. My hope is that by electing the best environmental president in American history, Al Gore, we can move forward."

It would be interesting to see how Pope deciphers flaws from failures.

And on May 11, 2004, before the Green Party even announced its support for a candidate, the Sierra Club had already endorsed John Kerry for president. "Now, thousands of Sierra Club members in every state will be volunteering their efforts to tell voters about the clear choice in this election," Larry Fahn, the Sierra Club's current president, said. "They will be encouraging all Americans who care about the environment to vote for John Kerry in November."

Throughout his career Kerry has received great marks from the Sierra Club for his purported environmental commitment. However, the Club's criteria for grading politicians is obviously lacking. A closer look at Kerry's real environmental report card yields a much different grade.

For starters, Kerry has never supported the Kyoto Protocol, and as he told *Grist Magazine* in a 2003 interview, "[The Kyoto agreement] doesn't ask enough of developing nations, the nations that are going to be producing much greater emissions and which we need to get on the right course now through technology transfer." Somebody should have mentioned to Kerry that despite the US accounting for only 4% of the world's population, we still emit over a quarter of the globe's carbon dioxide. But don't count on Kerry to call on the US to set an example for developing countries; that would be asking too much.

As previously noted, in 2003, Kerry decided not to cast a vote against a portion of Bush's chainsaw Forest Plan (HR 1904). This, combined with his support for Fast Track legislation, NAFTA, WTO, the bombing of Afghanistan, Iraq, along with his refusal to oppose hilltop strip mining, his intervention with the National Marine Fisheries Service when they attempted to restrict Cod fishing off the Outer Banks of North Carolina, and chemical fumigation in Colombia to counter coca and opium production—which destroys everything in its path—provides us with a clear warning that Kerry isn't an environmentalist, much less good at pretending to be one. In fact, Kerry's commitment to dropping chemicals on Colombia goes well beyond countenance.

Rand Beers, Kerry's national security advisor, is an ardent supporter of destroying Colombia's ecosystem through biowarfare.

As Sean Donahue wrote for *CounterPunch* in January 2004,

> Under Presidents Clinton and Bush, [Beers] served as Assistant Secretary of State for International Narcotics and Law Enforcement Affairs, and was one of the chief architects of and apologists for the United States' cruel policies in Colombia.
>
> Beers was most closely associated with the disastrous aerial crop fumigation program the US introduced in southern Colombia. The State Department hired DynCorp, a private military contractor, to fly crop dusters at high altitudes over the rainforests of southern Colombia, spraying a chemical cocktail that includes a stronger version of Monsanto's popular and controversial herbicide, Round-Up, over suspected coca fields. Beers was the public face of the fumigation program, defending and advocating for it in Congressional hearings and in the media.

Well, at least Kerry was never marinated in crude oil like Bush, you say? Not so fast there. Kerry in the summer of 2004 told Teamster's president Jimmy Hoffa that while he opposes drilling in the Alaskan National Wildlife Refuge, he has no qualms with drilling "everywhere else like never before." Where is this "everywhere?" How about the Powder River Basin in Wyoming, the red rocks in Utah, the Rocky Mountain flats, the coasts of Alaska and the Gulf of Mexico, just to name a few? Kerry, it seems, had no alternative energy plan whatsoever; he simply wanted to drill for more oil. Call Bush Kerry's mentor.

In the fall of 2004, Senator Kerry, weary from the campaign trail, took an afternoon off to spend time with the American Gas Association. At the elite gathering, Kerry, rubbing shoulders with oil execs, pledged his support for a Trans-Alaska-Canada Natural Gas Pipeline. This devastating conduit would cut across some of the most pristine wilderness and taiga in Canada, and by far the most untouched landscape in North America and perhaps the world. While the Trans-Alaska Pipeline is a modest creation next to Kerry's grand vision, the Senator still received fabulous ratings from the big environmental groups.

So why does the Club continue to pledge faithful allegiance to the Democratic Party?

Here's some insight:

Many Sierra Club board members give bundles to Democratic campaigns. Guy Saperstein, a member of the Club's board, gave $2,000 to John Kerry in 2000, and has donated in excess of $65,000 to other Democrats since that time. Another board member, Charles Frank, has given over $20,000 to Democrats in the past four years. Other members, including Al Meyerhoff, Robert B. Flint, and Robert J. Heil, have given cash to the Democrats for a combined total of $16,000.

Advisory member J. Fred Weintz even went so far as to help out the Bush election campaign in 2000, forking over $6,000 to the GOP, while fellow board member Robert B. Flint gave Republican John McCain $500. And the list goes on. It shouldn't come as much of a surprise, then, that year after year the Club backs mainstream candidates instead of supporting Green or more radical alternatives to the Democratic mainstream.

Backing Bush

On the eve of Bush's invasion of Iraq, the Sierra Club fell short in forcefully opposing the imminent war. The organization's leaders even threatened to fire any employees of the organization that dared to denounce the illegal offensive. These spineless enviros, most likely afraid of rocking the Democratic boat, must have known better, for the first Gulf War had devastating effects on the environment.

Over 700 oil wells were set ablaze by Iraqi soldiers when the US entered the conflict. Prior to this horrific atrocity, as CNN reported in 1999, "Iraq was responsible for intentionally releasing some 11 million barrels of oil into the Arabian Gulf from January to May 1991, oiling more than 800 miles of Kuwaiti and Saudi Arabian coastline. The amount of oil released was categorized as 20 times larger than the Exxon Valdez spill in Alaska and twice as large as the previous world record oil spill. The cost of cleanup has been estimated at more than $700 million."

The Club should have recognized such a disaster was likely to ensue as the US invaded Iraq. Saddam loyalists promised to light oil fields afire, hoping to expose what they claimed were the US's underlying motives for attacking their country—oil.

But the Iraqis weren't the only ones to blame for such environmental devastation during the first Gulf War. The US drowned at least 80 crude oil ships to the bottom of the Persian Gulf partly to uphold the UN's economic sanctions against Iraq in the early 1990s.

After studying the ecological effects of the war, Green Cross International wrote in a 2000 report:

> The detrimental impacts of coastal development on marine resources will not end in 15 years, but instead will be felt much longer, if not forever. The coast has been developed increasingly since the War, without environmental impact assessments in most of the cases. Also, several huge projects are planned for the future (e.g., completion of the waterfront project, the bridge across Kuwait Bay, free trade zone on Bubiyan Island). Thorough examination needs to be undertaken to identify the risks posed to marine life by these coastal development projects ... The environmental impact of air pollution fallout, fumes, and desert topsoil contamination

from the oil lakes may have long-term health consequences through accumulation in the food chain or contamination of irrigation and drinking water. They represent a major long-term public health issue because they potentially affect the whole population of Kuwait. Research and monitoring efforts should be directed to further assess exposure levels and health outcomes. The role of ongoing environmental pollution from industrial sources (e.g. pollution from traffic and oil industries) and behavioral health co-factors (e.g. diet, smoking) also ought to be assessed.

With all this information on the first Iraq war, the Sierra Club still couldn't say no to Bush's war. But some vocal chapters of the Club did voice their opposition to the invasion. The San Francisco Bay and New Mexico chapters, for instance, protested after several Sierra Club activists paved the way in Glen Canyon Utah. "The present administration has declared its intention to achieve total military dominance of the world," Patrick Diehl, vice-chair of the Glen Canyon Group, told *CounterPunch* during the height of their dissent. "We believe that such ambitions will produce a state of perpetual war, undoing whatever protection of the environment … conservation groups may have so far achieved."

In response Sierra Club president Ferenstein gave a tepid rebuttal in the *Christian Science Monitor*. "In order to reduce oil's influence in geopolitical relations," she wrote, "the US and other nations have to move away from an oil-dependent economy toward a future based on clean energy, greater efficiency and more renewable power. The Sierra Club has called for a peaceful resolution of the conflict in Iraq, proceeding according to the UN resolutions, and we emphatically believe that long-term stability depends on the US reducing our oil dependence."

Responding to these assertions, St. Clair argued, "Apparently, Ferenstein doesn't understand that the UN Resolution gives the US and Britain the green light to whack Iraq with the slightest provocation, real or fabricated. And apparently war is okay with the Club as long as it's the result of a consensus process (even if the UN consensus was brokered by bullying and bribery)—although how the environment suffers any less under this feel-good scenario remains a mystery."

As the wound inflicted by insurgent Club members who opposed the war began to bleed, Ferenstein reluctantly declared the Sierra Club opposed the "United States' military action against Iraq." It was too little too late. The Club, after all, should have been on the front lines protesting Bush's illegal invasion of Iraq from the very start.

The Sierra Club had failed to take the Republicans and the Democrats to task. By doing so the Club actually helped weaken Democratic opposition to the Republican's atrocious policies. This weakness, in turn, allowed Bush to get away with virtually everything he pleased. Including the Iraq invasion.

Chapter Sixteen

Kerry's Pummeling Not a Surprise

Bush with a TKO

Yaaaawn. It is November 3, the day after George W. Bush won his reelection campaign. No, I am not exhausted because I stayed up into the wee hours of the morning glaring into a fuzzy TV set watching the polls roll in. I am just bored. John Kerry phoned George Bush earlier today to concede the race and gave his lifeless concession speech later in the afternoon.

The Democratic elite are not going to wage a fight over the Ohio electorate, where the vote split is greater than 136,000, even though some 150,000 absentee ballots have yet to be counted and voting fraud is fast making its way into the headlines. But if the tables were turned, you can bet the Republicans would have flown James Baker out to Ohio to begin the recount and wring the necks of some Democratic operatives. The Democrats aren't much for fighting, as we well know, so no alarms have been sounded.

Anyway, Bush not only kicked Kerry's butt in Ohio. He also slapped him around in Florida, where the vote margin for Bush exceeded 376,000 votes. Luckily, the spread was such that Ralph Nader's measly 32,000 votes in the Sunshine State could not be blamed for Kerry's brow beating. The Democrats proved unequivocally that they can lose all on their own.

Given that Nader's presence in 2004 hardly aided Bush's victory at all, it looks like all the time and millions of dollars spent by Democrats and their liberal cohorts to keep Ralph off the ballot were all for naught. Not to mention an awful strategy. In fact, some of the sultry attacks on Nader came from the same group of funders who drove Howard Dean out of the primary race.

Many of these DC opportunists came together to form

Naderfactor.org, which begged Nader not to run, and then attempted to smear his character once he defied their plea by announcing his candidacy to Tim Russert on *Meet the Press*. It should be noted that the president of the Naderfactor was Tricia Enright, the Dean campaign's former communications director, who transitioned herself with ease from the Dean camp to the dark Kerry quarters. No qualms were raised. What a waste.

Enright wasn't the only Democrat working to silence Nader. In fact, a fair number of the Kerrycrats were behind the "dirty tricks" to keep Nader off the ballot in swing states this year.

Writing for LeftHook.org in early October, Toby Shepard had this to say about the shenanigans:

> Take Oregon. After Nader volunteers collected more than the required 15,306 signatures (a total of 18,186) needed to appear on the state's ballot, Secretary of State Bill Bradbury invented reasons to disqualify his constituents. If signatures appeared illegible, (despite printed names appearing directly below 'illegible' signatures) Bradbury disqualified them. In one instance, a volunteer had begun to write a '7' to mark the day of the month, realized the error, crossed it out and wrote '8.' Bradbury discarded the entire sheet. Bradbury even threw out 2,354 signatures (which had already been verified by individual counties) because they were submitted without page numbers. All in all, Bradbury left Nader 218 signatures short of being on the state ballot. Three cheers for democracy.
>
> In Pennsylvania, a law firm by the name of Reed Smith successfully barred Nader from appearing on the state's ballot. According to the *Washington Post*, the firm (whose PAC gives primarily to the RNC) counsels 29 of the top 30 US banks, 26 of the Fortune 50 companies, 9 of the top 10 pharmaceutical companies and 50 of the world's largest leading drug and medical device manufactures. *The New York Times* quoted one lawyer as saying '8 to 10 lawyers in

[the] firm were working pro bono on the case, 80 hours each a week for two weeks.'

In Arizona, large Democratic donors employed the services of three corporate law firms to file frivolous challenges to Nader's ample number of signatures. 1,349 signatures were thrown out because the volunteer who had collected them failed to provide the correct name of the county, despite filling out the rest of their address accurately.

In Ohio, the law firm of Kirkland and Ellis (of which Kenneth Starr is a partner), whose former clients include Dow Corning (breast implant litigation), Brown and Williamson Tobacco (anti-smoking cases brought by state attorney generals), and General Motors (product defect cases against victims of injuries), has provided two full-time lawyers to keep Nader-Camejo off the ballot.

This is what democracy looks like. The Democrats should have used their money and energy to register voters in Florida and Ohio instead. Or better yet, allocated those funds to make the case for voting pro-Democrat as opposed to anti-Republican. Then again, there were not many exciting things to say about Senator Kerry, aside from a few snide jokes regarding his botoxed cheeks and perfectly groomed mane.

No doubt we should have seen the writing on the wall back in July when the Democratic National Convention proved to be nothing more than a glorified war parade, with Kerry floating by reprehensibly announcing he was "reporting for duty."

Since Kerry's ambiguous proclamation in Boston last summer he has trounced around the country defending his call for the continued US occupation of Iraq. In Florida during the first presidential debate, Kerry even boasted of his numerous veteran military backers, "I am proud that important military figures are supporting me in this race: former Chairman of the Joint Chiefs of Staff John Shalikashvili; just yesterday, General Eisenhower's son, General John Eisenhower, endorsed me; General Admiral

William Crowe; General Tony McBeak, who ran the Air Force war so effectively for his father—all believe I would make a stronger commander-in-chief."

With Kerry singing such a militaristic tune, it should come as no surprise that *The New York Times'* former conservative columnist William Safire dubbed Kerry the "newest neo-conservative" who is even "more hawkish than President Bush," on October 4, 2004.

Safire, no doubt, was right on the mark. When Kerry sought to show voters that he would have been tough on terror, for instance, he did so by defending Bush's preemptive policy. "The president always has the right, and always has had the right, for preemptive strike. That was a great doctrine throughout the Cold War. And it was always one of the things we argued about with respect to arms control."

So much for distancing himself from the Bush agenda. No wonder the Democrats were more energized *against* Nader than *for* Kerry. If anything, Kerry was simply saying he could do the whole thing better, and in fact did say as much. "[I] will hunt and kill the terrorists wherever they are," Kerry belted out in the first presidential debate. "I can do better." Kerry also said he would accomplish his goal by not backing off "of Fallujah and other places," which, he proclaimed, "[sends] the wrong message to terrorists."

So much for options in 2004. Lefty voters were told that they had to vote for a pro-war candidate. There was no choice. Period. We were all left out, and that makes me wonder: What ever happened to the anti-war movement anyway? You'd think they would have raised some hell over Kerry's hawkish pose on Iraq. Maybe these seasoned activists have been on a nice vacation, or out campaigning for Kerry since his nomination. Talk about hypocrites. We'll see what kind of credibility they'll have now that they are getting back to work.

Predictably, Election Day was by and large a miserable venture for the Democrats—and not just in the presidential race. Along with Kerry, who plotted his own demise, South Dakota's veteran Democratic Senator Tom Daschle, went down in flames to his handsome younger challenger, John Thune. The Republicans, with the help of Tom Delay's redistricting in Texas, also extended their 12-year reign of control in the House of Representatives.

The Dems did manage to pull out a few wins, however, including the great triumph of Cynthia McKinney in Georgia and Barack Obama's landslide victory in the Illinois Senate race against right-wing radio personality Alan Keyes. Young Obama is often referred to as the new hope to transform the Democratic Party into a progressive powerhouse.

His speech at the Democratic National Convention was said by some to have outshined that of Howard Dean and even Bill Clinton. But like Dean, Obama should not be mistaken for a progressive. Just one day after he stole the spotlight at the convention, Obama told reporters, "On Iraq, on paper, there's not as much difference, I think, between the Bush administration and a Kerry administration as there would have been a year ago." He added, "There's not that much difference between my position and George Bush's position at this stage. The difference, in my mind, is who's in a position to execute."

Writing for *CounterPunch*, Eric Ruder said of Obama: "[He] is a gifted politician. Like Bill Clinton, he knows how to encourage people of opposite political beliefs to see what they want to see in his speeches and policy prescriptions … Obama finds a way to talk left—but makes it clear that he will never pose a threat to corporate interests or make a policy proposal that would carry a hefty price tag. In Illinois, where it's obvious that the death penalty system is too flawed to fix, Obama is celebrated by liberals as a crusader for death penalty reform—but he continues to support capital punishment for 'punishing the most heinous crimes.'"

Ruder adds, "Obama calls for tax breaks for American workers and government measures to create jobs. But he's a supporter of Corporate America's 'free trade' agenda ... Obama claims to be a defender of the public school system who will campaign to put more teachers in classrooms. But he also trumpets charter schools—with their record of union-busting and siphoning funds from public schools."

Much like Howard Dean did for a fleeting period, Obama's victory has given many progressive Democrats reason to believe that change may be on the way for their party. Change is certainly on its way, but how fruitful it will be remains to be seen. To be sure, you can expect a fight within the Democratic chambers in the months and years ahead, as Joe Trippi warned on *Now with Bill Moyers*. Trippi, who told Moyers the Dean movement isn't dead yet, suggested, "I think what's gonna happen is the first initial response is gonna be to reform the Democratic Party from within."

In fact, Dean's progressive funds helped elect Democratic Governor Brian Schweitzer (who ran with a Republican as his Lieutenant Governor) in the state of Montana, which is a conservative bastion. Dean's organization, Democracy for America (DFA), which he formed after dropping out of the primaries, helped elect a total of 31 democratic candidates in 2004, 15 of which will be first-time office holders.

However, the looming fight within the Democratic Party may be a wasted effort. For it will be waged not by true progressives like Dennis Kucinich, but by purported progressives like Obama and Dean. We know what happened to Dean as well as Kucinich in the primaries, and you can rest assured that any fight for policy "change," even if waged by centrists, will again be muted much like Dean was this election season. The Democratic establishment will surely look at Kerry's loss and pump up their rhetorical machine to call for the Democrats' continued attempt to outflank the Republicans to the right—even though this strategy has been a losing one for years.

As Al Sharpton told *Playboy* during the Democratic primary race, "This whole centrist move, which I consider a Right move, hasn't worked politically. Centrists keep saying we can't win without going to the center. Well, they have been in charge of the party since 1992. It's 11 years later, and we have lost everything. We lost the House in 1994 with Gingrich, and we failed to regain it in 1996, 1998, 2000, and 2002. How do you lose five Super Bowls and not say there is something wrong with this coach and this game plan? Aside from the fact that I don't believe in what they are saying—pro-death penalty, pro-business deregulation, pro-NAFTA—politically it hasn't even worked. They act as though they are outsiders shooting at the inside. They are the insiders. They have control of the party, and they have failed. They have put this party on its deathbed."

While the losses may seem to be coming to a head just now, the Democrats have been lying in their current state for quite some time.

Consider, for instance, Jesse Jackson's populist Rainbow Coalition, which took on the Beltway establishment in the 1980s. Once Clinton took the helm in 1992, the group had little to show for their arduous efforts. "By a brisk accounting of 1993 to 2000, the black stripe of the Rainbow got the Crime Bill, women got 'welfare reform,' labor got NAFTA, gays and lesbians got the Defense of Marriage Act. Even with a Democratic Congress in the early years, the peace crowd got no cuts in the military; unions got no help on the right to organize; advocates of DC statehood got nothing (though statehood would virtually guarantee two more Democratic Senate seats and more representation in the House); the single-payer crowd got worse than nothing." As Jo Ann Wypijewski writes in *Dime's Worth of Difference: Beyond the Lesser of Two Evils*, "Between Clinton's inauguration and the day he left office, 700,000 more persons were incarcerated, mostly minorities; today, one in eight black men is barred from voting because of prison, probation, or parole."

In short, as on so many other issues, the Democratic Party disarms its progressive wing in order to enable a rightward move. It should be clear to any would-be-challenger that the Democratic Party is not open to the politics supported by its base—minorities, the poor, and unions.

This democratic shortcoming, along with Kerry's failure to inspire the American electorate, explains why the Democrats faltered in 2004, despite a seemingly massive grassroots undertaking to oust Bush. With November 2 as evidence, it is safe to say that hatred for an incumbent is not enough to elect a challenger. Bush was and is hated, no doubt. But many who supported John Kerry were uninspired by his campaign. For he failed to distinguish himself from his Republican opponent on a range of issues—from war to the economy, from trade to civil liberties. It was textbook "lesser-evilism," and as was the case in so many elections before, it was a losing strategy. Democrats must learn to offer alternatives if they ever want to win. But don't count on them for that.

Kerry's campaign was also consistently in a tailspin. Jeffrey St. Clair and Alexander Cockburn summed it up nicely after Kerry's concession:

> Week after week Kerry and his boosters displayed an unmatched deafness to political tone. The haughty elitist from Boston probably lost most of the Midwest forever when he said in the high summer that foreign leaders hoped he would win. The applause of the French in Cannes for Michael Moore's *9/11* was the sound of the cement drying over the corpse of Kerry's chances of carrying the Midwest. Soros's dollars were like flowers on the grave ...
> If there was a visual premonition of why George Bush

would achieve a popular majority beyond challenge, it was probably the photographs of gay couples celebrating their marriages outside San Francisco's city hall. America is a very Christian country ... October surprises? No candidate was more burdened by them than George Bush. Just in the last couple of weeks, headlines brought tidings of US marines killed in Baghdad and other US troops rising up in mutiny against lack of equipment to protect their lives. The president's brother Neil was exposed as influence-peddling on the basis of his family connections. The economic numbers remained grim as they have been all year. And this was just the icing on the cake. You can troll back over the past fifteen months and find scarcely a headline or news story bringing good tidings for Bush. History is replete with revolutions caused by a rise in the price of bread. This year the price of America's primal fluid—oil—on which every household depends, tripled.

But Kerry and the Democrats were never able to capitalize on any of these headlines, a failure which started when Democrats in Congress, Kerry included, gave the green light to the war on Iraq, and which continued when Kerry conclusively threw away the war and WMD issues in August. When he tried to do a chord change at NYU on September 20, it was too late, and even then his position remained incoherent. He offered no way out. More tunnel, no light.

When all the hype about the "youth vote," "e-activism," "buses to Ohio," and "house DVD parties" withered away so tragically and so pathetically on Election Day 2004—and with devout Kerry-Edwards supporters battling denial—the only leftist forces remaining were the Anti-Anybody-But-Bush crew. Not surprisingly, the anti-ABBers were feeling vindicated.

The Gangrene Party

The Green Party, which unfortunately fell victim to the plague of ABB, opted to run a safe-state campaign. Although Green Party presidential candidate David Cobb did not call what he did a "safe-state" approach, reality suggests that this was exactly the approach his team took. Cobb admitted time and again that his campaign planned on focusing on states that were safely in either Bush or Kerry's camps, not states that could swing the election one way or the other.

According to his official website in October 2004: "[Cobb] has said he will focus his campaign on states neglected by the corporate parties (i.e. 'safe-states'), he has also said that he will visit and campaign in any state that invites him ... For example, [Cobb] has pledged to visit the battleground states like Ohio and Pennsylvania to support their petition drives to put the Green Party candidate on the state ballots."

In other words, Cobb would not actively campaign for his own candidacy in swing states even if he were on the ballot. He would, however, continue to work in those states for other Green hopefuls.

"[In swing] states, I'm acknowledging that there is a profound responsibility on the citizens," Cobb told Steve Curwood in an NPR interview.

After Cobb announced that he wanted Pat LaMarche to be his running mate, the not-so-primetime radio personality from Maine said she would not commit to voting for herself and Cobb in November's election.

"If Bush has got 11 percent of the vote in Maine come November 2, I can vote for whoever I want," she told the *Portland Press Herald/Maine Sunday Telegram*. Translation: if the polls in Maine were close, LaMarche said she might ever so selflessly vote for Kerry instead of the Green ticket. "If the race is close I'll vote for Kerry ... I love my country ... [and] if [Vice President] Dick Cheney loved his country, he wouldn't be voting for himself."

Later, perhaps realizing the futility of her remarks, LaMarche posted a press release on the Cobb campaign website, lamenting: "I am honored to be the Green Party vice presidential candidate running with David Cobb. I want to reassure all members of the Green Party that, on November 2, I will be voting Cobb/ LaMarche."

But it was too late. The cat was out of the bag. LaMarche, like Cobb, believed Kerry offered a stark alternative to Bush's band of neo-cons. Unfortunately, Cobb and the Greens did not realize that you cannot effectively pressure the Democrats or a candidate like John Kerry if you declare you might vote for him sans specific demands. Lamarche's role as a candidate should have been to campaign as hard as she could in an effort to build the Green Party, leaving strategic choices to the voters.

Of course, David Cobb insisted that he was unconcerned with his vote count, telling me in an interview that his vote tally was "one of the least important indicators of support" for his campaign. As he explained, "In our first presidential campaign in 1996, Ralph Nader received less than 1% of the vote, and I think it's safe to say that we did not become politically irrelevant afterwards." But Cobb failed to mention that Nader's 1996 bid—which Nader himself doesn't even consider a presidential run since he didn't campaign—marked the Greens' first real stab at a presidential election. They had nowhere to go but up. Not the case in 2004.

The bottom line? Cobb failed to step into the ring, let alone lace up his gloves. First, he ran for the Green Party's nomination using what he called a "safe-state" approach, where he would not focus his energy on those states that could put pressure on Kerry.

What Cobb and most Greens do not realize is that they

inadvertently helped reelect Bush by giving Kerry a get-out-of-jail-free card. If the Greens had put more pressure on Kerry, the Democrat may have taken stronger positions and effectively differentiated himself from the Republicans.

The Greens could, and should, have been vociferously opposing the war in Iraq and Afghanistan. They should have been on the frontlines of the campaign scene, denouncing Kerry and Bush's neoliberalism and their handling of the downward economic spiral, civil liberties infringements, and environmental catastrophes. But instead they caved—and paid a steep price, getting pounded at the polls. A miserable sixth place.

Cobb and LaMarche earned a little over 118,000 votes on November 2, 2004. Even though only half a million people voted for Nader in 2004—a drastic decline compared to four years earlier when 2.8 million people voted Green—Ralph Nader still managed to garner five times as many votes as his former party's ticket on November 2, 2004, despite being vilified by the left and the Democrats.

Many cite the drastic reduction in votes for Nader in 2004 as evidence of failure. But it is wrong to compare the two runs in these terms. In the second case, Nader had no party to back him, and in the wake of 9/11 hysteria, many who were with Nader in spirit decided to cast their votes for Kerry in hopes of unseating Bush.

Nader was also denied ballot access in a dozen states. The Libertarian Party, which garnered some 200,000 more votes than the Greens, put it to the Greens, too. Looks like the Greens and Cobb got their wish. For they had never wanted those votes anyway.

An example of the ruin: In Minnesota, the Green Party has enjoyed majority status since 2000, but is now heading back to the political fringe. Cobb's poor vote total disqualified the Greens from $400,000 in public subsidies and automatic ballot access in the state. Looks like they will have to start over from scratch in the state, as well as Connecticut, Montana, Utah, Nevada, New Mexico, and Rhode Island, where the Green Party lost the presidential ballot access they had acquired during the 2000 election. They also lost Nebraska, which they obtained in July 2004.

And you thought black Tuesday was the death-knell of the Democrats alone. Truth be told, the Greens may prove to be more damaged when this year's battle ashes finally settle. Cobb and the Greens now regrettably signify the politics of mendacity. Picking up the pieces of their shattered foundation won't be easy—if at all possible.

What's Next?

So what's to be done? The Democrats and John Kerry clearly failed us, as did the Green Party, which was the largest progressive party in the United States up until 2004.

Code Pink co-founder and Green Party loyalist Medea Benjamin, who supported David Cobb's disappointing campaign, may have hit the nail on the head in *The Nation* when she denounced her decision to champion the safe-state strategy in 2004:

> Many of us in the Green Party made a tremendous compromise by campaigning in swing states for such a miserable standard-bearer for the progressive movement as John Kerry. Well, I've had it. As George Bush says, "Fool me once, shame on you. Fool me—you can't get fooled again."
>
> For those of you willing to keep wading in the muddy waters of the Democratic Party, all power to you. I plan to work with the Greens to get more Green candidates elected to local office.

Whether it is the Green Party or another third party that rises to challenge the Democrats and Republicans, an unyielding force must be cultivated if we ever want to see a political entity in

Washington represent our concerns.

This political body must be akin to the Greens in 2000, when their candidate Ralph Nader took on the establishment with full force, regardless of the alleged consequences. Such a third party will have to be uncompromising in its vigor, intent, and stamina. The process will take years. That means the David Cobb safe-state strategy must be abolished, for it serves absolutely no purpose but to validate a corrupt system.

Never again should a third party surrender to the logic of lesser-evilism. It's time to let the voters decide. And let's provide those voters with many new voices and choices.

Those millions of non-voters must be given reasons to go to the polls. They must be given real options and guided in a new direction—far off the Democrats' and Republicans' current collision course.

Some will inevitably continue to recommend reforming the Democratic Party from within. Many Nader bashers and ABBers adopted such a line in 2004, claiming that if Nader had only run as a Democratic candidate for the party's presidential nomination, he could do oh-so-much to influence its direction. Yet the examples of Howard Dean and Dennis Kucinich have shown us that such attempts produce nothing short of relentless attacks, backstabbing, and silencing.

Let us hope that the left and those who fell victim to the misguided "Anybody But Bush" epidemic this year outgrow their naïveté in elections to come. Not only did the ABB phenomenon reflect poor reasoning, it also helped reelect Bush. Kerry, consequently, was only accountable to the party bigwigs and not those voters and citizens on the ground fighting for change, regardless of who is in office. Had Kerry been accountable to we the people, the popular vote spread would not have been some 3.3 million votes in favor of George W. Bush.

Index

Author Biographies

Joshua Frank was born and raised in Billings, Montana, and now lives in Albany, New York. His work has appeared in many publications, among them: *CounterPunch*, *Z Magazine*, *Clamor*, *Green Left Weekly*, *AVA Oregon*, and *Earth First! Journal*. He also contributed an essay to *Dime's Worth of Difference: Beyond the Lesser of Two Evils*, published by CounterPunch/AK Press in September 2004.

Jeffrey St. Clair is the co-editor of *CounterPunch* with Alexander Cockburn. He is the author of many books, including *Been Brown So Long it Looked Like Green to Me: The Politics of Nature*, published by Common Courage Press in March 2004. He resides in Oregon City, Oregon.

Sunil K. Sharma is a musician and editor of DissidentVoice. org, an online newsletter "dedicated to challenging the distortions and lies of the corporate press and the privileged classes it serves." He lives in Northern California.

Merlin Chowkwanyun is a radio personality, journalist, and rabble-rouser. His work has appeared in many publications including the *Pasadena Weekly*, *Dissident Voice* and *CounterPunch*. He currently resides in New York City.